CAPTURED IN A LIFE CASE FOR TRUTH

WHAT LIES WITHIN

Lisa Leikam

CAPTURED IN A LIFE CASE FOR TRUTH

This book's contents are solely the experiences and opinions of the author's experiences and research and are not to be taken in any way as professional medical advice. If you require professional help, please call your local medical or hospital provider.

ISBN: 978-0578820927

TABLE OF CONTENTS

PART I

THE JOURNEY...9

PART II

DISCOVERY...57

Poetry by Lisa

TO YOU, THE READER…

WITH LOVE, FAITH & BELIEF

The meaning of life is to find your gift,

the purpose of life is to give it away.

Pablo Picasso

INTRODUCTION

It was the 1980s when I was positive I'd found life's purpose. Unfortunately, it wasn't being a newly wedded wife. It wasn't having children and raising a family. Those were contributors to life, but they were not a purpose.

Sadly, my purpose was appearing to be paying medical bills. Up until getting married, those were not my concern. My parents paid for them. Now, in marriage, my husband and I were responsible for our medical insurance and medical bills. It was for better or worse, right?

The expenses from my chronic health issues, tests, and hospitalizations, became a monthly budget. It was then I was confident I was put here on Earth, in purpose, to pay medical bills.

Illnesses and disease can be prevalent throughout anyone's life. Some with unknown causes, or cures. Many unseen, and unbeknownst to others. Anxiety, unresolved trauma, and fear and depression are upon the unseen, unspoken, or unknown—a truth of life, which is not apparent by others.

This was me, my life, until my brother Lenny's passing in 2015. After that, love from spirit, spirit guides, angels, and my Creator, comforted me, surrounded me, captured me and healed me.

While there had been no cure in the past, only medications, I removed the chronic internal health diseases, and pain and medications that came with it. A miracle in itself.

I also played the odds, gambling for answers, to a meaning of the mystical human form I found etched on the side of my trash can (This I have named a "totem of souls").

Made of ashes, in an unknown justification, it becomes a lifeline in purpose, of a spiritual healing journey—a miraculous and astonishing life experience in a truth of enlightenment and a purpose. The truth is mind-blowing.

THE JOURNEY

Part I

A DIFFICULT TASK

It was September 2017. As I sat in the small compact waiting room, with only four seating chairs, reading the quote I coincidentally opened a book page to, my mind gave off a silent "no duh" reaction. My inner voice inside my head told me I already knew what it was saying. I honestly did not require this sign, a written message, confirming it.

It was an annual business review appointment. I'd driven the short trip to town and arrived for my 3:00 p.m. appointment. I took a seat next to the small round table in the corner of the waiting room. On the table sat the miniature-sized book. The name, "The Complete Life's Little Instruction Book."

I retrieved the book. Appropriately, I thought, considering I was in the depth of learning all about life and lessons. I opened the book generically, which was in the middle. The pages showed Volume Two at the top. The first quote on the right-hand page was No. 801. It said, "Become famous for finishing important, difficult tasks."

As I sat there that day, reading the quote, my inner voice told me I already knew it. I knew I had yet another difficult task ahead. That task was the next book, as it was revealing its difficulties as well. It would take revealing personal insecurities, anxieties, and chronic lifelong health diseases.

Life had been everything, but ordinary, or simple, since the initial release of *Captured by the Holy Spirit* in November 2015. Or should I say, since my brother Lenny's passing.

Time produced additional "Alice in Wonderland" mystical, magical, fantasy type days after that. Because by noon, I could've experienced any amount of impossible things. Yes, nothing was normal. Receiving signs from Heaven was simply beautiful, and healing, except there was this unknown.

I was self-confident with the new energy I had; in myself, my thoughts, intuition, and faith. I was trusting the journey and found peace in that, and myself. I was going with the daily process and flow of life.

Initially though, I was hit with a tidal wave, forcing me across an enormous vast open ocean. I yearned for a lifeboat no one could, or would, provide. Religious representatives, philosophers, and specialty physicians I contacted were near unresponsive.

I'd fretted in where life had taken me. Life as I knew it was gone. I was working through awakening, the dark night of my soul. Life was all about lessons; I was learning. There was no easy way through it. It was a day to day process.

Up to now, my time involved professionalizing *Captured by the Holy Spirit*. The initial release was an authentic Indie piece of work. It now needed to be professionalized. It needed an editor and designer. And it required completion.

Completed, in the initial online release, the most significant revelation, in my trashcan, made of cigarette ashes, had not been written into the story. The human formed figure discovered was left out. I truthfully wasn't sure what the mysterious, "human-formed-figure" meant, or how it appeared.

As additional signs, synchronicities, and "coincidences" from Heaven and the Universe occurred, my memorabilia was mounting up. The other desk in our office was accumulating and compiling an extensive collection of feathers, coins, rocks, cards, material, and photos. The trash can with the 'totem of souls', sat on the floor next to it.

It wasn't that I feared my journey. I was confident in the miraculous events and the transformation of my mind, body, spirit, and health; and who was leading it. It was physically and mentally evident; in my grief, I found a new inner light.

The nervousness and anxiety I carried were being removed—a plague since early childhood. Antidepressants, benzodiazepines, acid blockers, and lifelong symptoms were vanishing. A cure longed for and desired. All gently calmed and removed.

Now, I knew I was experiencing a life "case" in purpose. The verbal Petition I pled was filed in *Captured by the Holy Spirit.*

In Philippians 4:6, He states:

"Do not be anxious about anything, but in every situation, by prayer and petition, with thanksgiving, present your requests to God."

This I had done.

In light of what I was experiencing and discovering, the nature of my experience is one of a spiritual awakening. The personal experiences, mystical coincidences, and revelations are God's grace, coming in a time of despair.

A personal spiritual awakening can come from a time of loss, confusion, and fear, in which God enters one's heart. He awakens the soul and awareness in and around them. He captures one, filling them with His guidance, knowledge, and love.

I knew my next journey; in writing the next book, it would take getting personal on an intimate level. To continue, in writing, would take revealing life-long battles in health—my fears, anxiety, and forever, internally, diseased life.

Here I was, a simplistic, simple-minded, yet relatively knowledgeable, Catholic girl, wading in the depth of life and death, in faith. Experiences and spirit were leading me into my life case discovery. As I sit here, the development is ongoing. There was no looming deadline this time.

There was only one day at a time—moment by moment. I was learning, and time was in the now and present. There was no need to stress. It had all been working out so far—all in divine timing. I appreciated all that I was at this moment.

I always thought it would be fun to be an investigator. I believe that's what I loved most about being a legal assistant. There was research. I was forever looking to uncover and find evidence, to reveal the truth of a mystery. It was an exciting career.

Now I found myself that investigator, a case of truth-seeking in what had appeared before me. Willpower was a strong point. I had no problem in completing a difficult task or project. Those who know me, know that's true.

You don't give a girl with fire in her soul, a mind of determination, perfection, and completion, a task not to be completed. But this task, as I now knew, would be as challenging as the last.

SPIRITUAL AWAKENING

A spiritual awakening can be described as having a profound personal experience after a difficult event in life; a divorce, a diagnosis, an abusive relationship, a childhood trauma, a death, a financial crisis, or other hardship and life-altering event that takes someone to the depth of their soul.

Confused and frightened, their outer self is exposed, and the inner self is cracked open. The personal ego is challenged, sorting through the internal and external repercussions experienced and taught in life. One finds themself alone, vulnerable, and searching for answers.

In continuous spirited efforts, one learns and understands the depth of life, love, family, forgiveness; and a contract, or purpose, in life. In the process, through faith, you are lifted up and captured by the higher divine source—your Creator.

A plea desperately requested, prayed for, and essential to salvation is answered. One is led to finding oneself through their inner light, inner voice, and self-power. Something they have no idea exists. One learns to trust in themselves, their intuition, faith, and the universal guidance of their higher power.

Awakening is a time of learning of oneself. One finds they never knew of self-love because no one taught them. One learns what was taught, told, and experienced plays into every aspect of life's reality and wellbeing.

It's a time of discovery of intuition and your inner voice. The voice silently in your mind, speaking through danger signs, truths, and internal senses, recognizing wrong and negativity. This inner voice is seeking to keep one safe from harm, as well.

On one side, the voice is your egotistical self, which pushes oneself into self-obsessions, judgments, selfishness, unkindness, and addictions in life. It is the side of the brain, which continually attacks and judges. This, the fear, devilish side.

The other side is the spiritual side. The good side. The angelic side, guiding us to love, joy, happiness, caring, empathy, and compassion. It is the spirit-within side, helping us in the right direction, guiding us.

Awakening teaches listening to the voice inside and deciphering the voices between good and evil, fear, and love. In learning to listen to the inner voice, the intuition also said to be your spirit guides, guardian angels, and your higher self; you learn to rely on and interact with it.

You learn to live and love on your own without expecting it back in return. Because, in truth, you won't receive what you need, for your inner-wellbeing. For in your efforts, you begin to understand, your intuition is the one you can depend upon. To keep you going safely, climbing, in your newest light within.

It shows you and leads you forward. It is referenced; life is written in a well and orchestrated script that only God can perform, mastered with completeness before one arrives. As if a script from a play, or movie, in which you have the part. Your birth, your character, your path, all uniquely planned out before you arrive.

As a person, you were created in an image here for a reason. Not for yourself or I; but for others. And there's this thing called a "purpose." Did you know you have a purpose, a spiritual purpose? A preplanned goal, or destination, in life. While it is a common saying, "everything happens for a reason," do you find yourself believing, maybe it's true? The information I've read in books, and articles, state the time of birth, and death, is placed upon us before arriving. My findings also stated our gender, parents, siblings, color, race, and talents are custom-made for our specific life journey and purpose.

In life, each of us has a unique spiritual purpose, each with our own specific role, personal challenges, or life lessons, which are carefully aligned with us. Everyone we meet is with purpose. Put onto our path, life lessons, and experiences.

Awakening takes you inward, to your inner self, your inner child, and spirit. One comes to learn on their own through the awakening, born-again, darkness to light transformation. You are learning of false stigmas placed upon us by society, family, ancestors, TV, media, shows, and ourselves. All of which are mind-controlling and affect our physical, mental, and emotional health.

I'd begun to learn and understand how stigma affected me, my mind, spirit, and health. We didn't come into life to be miserable, anxious, and worry.

The Creator tells us, do not be anxious, in 1 Peter 5:6-7; "Humble yourselves, therefore, under God's mighty hand, that he may lift you up in due time. Cast all your anxiety on him because he cares for you."

I found myself being guided by my inner-self, my faith, and my Creator, who brought me to this place. I was following, not for anyone, but for myself. In doing so, I gained independence in myself, in life, healing, and purpose. But first, I had to go through a shedding, darkness, into the releasement of the very being of who I was to me, in what I thought.

I let go of events and attachments which no longer served me—releasing personal judgments, past and current opinions, blame, and negative drama. Forgiveness became my daily pattern. I became attuned to an appreciation of all that was, all that I had, and allowed for fresh and positive energy to align with me. Do you realize energy is an enormous life force in our physical, emotional, and spiritual bodies?

Heredity, genetics, family traits throughout generations are imposed on us and our health. Hence, I got it from my dad. He's like his mother. The bloodlines and DNA are a large part of our being, holding us, our livelihood, our health, and our wellbeing captive.

Through awakening, one is guided to remove judgment, worry, self-doubt, and heredity attachments. In return, healing begins to manifest from the inside out. The small flickering glow, the suppressed light that once was dull, lethargic, and weak, comes to shine and glow within. A new fire is ignited in life.

So, it was after my brother's suicide, in February 2015, my spiritual awakening launched me onto a life discovery course. The nature of asking God for a sign, receiving "Flowers from Heaven" succumbed me.

My life was viewed from a new angle, and another language, with God, the Universe, angels, and spirit. The talking angel numbers, and signs, were God and the Universe's language. I aligned with a world of synchronicities and coincidences too large to ignore. And I was trusting my gut, myself, my faith, and my God.

Awakening will take you through life's memory lane; into memories, good and bad. Releasement, forgiveness, and self-love affirmations are life energy and health changers. I came to understand a greater magnitude of my mind and soul and the power with which it affected me.

Thoughts, emotions, beliefs, and words would be my key to unlock my deep inner turmoil. What we put into the mind, and believe, is what we receive. What we think is what becomes a reality. Positively and negatively. This, in light of a single, powerful word. A word society doesn't recognize or understand in its magnitude.

THE RELEASE

It was Friday, November 13, 2015. I awoke for work early that morning to find the email in my inbox. *Captured by the Holy Spirit* was now live on Amazon. After the extended late-night hours, the past week, writing, re-writing, editing, proofing, reproofing, and difficulties formatting and aligning the vast number of photos, it was now a published e-book. It was online and available to the entire world and universe. Good God, we did it!

At work, I went through the motions. My physical appearance portrayed I was there, but in truth, I was away. Away in the mystical realm of what life had brought and what'd transpired. Not only in light of the morning's email, but throughout the last ten months.

The day brought emotions and truth, of where my brother Lenny's suicide had taken me. Through it, I'd written a book. Two, honestly. All driven in belief and faith, with a message to share. It was a whirlwind destination in a short period of time.

The numbers, the hearts, and magically guided and timely coincidences had me believing the angels, God, and the Universe were guiding my soul and me. It was odd; the temperature outside that day was 65 degrees. Yet, the temperature reading in my car read 33 degrees. It read the same at lunch, and when I got off at 4:00 p.m. It appeared the number 33 was talking to me today.

In my book publishing research, I found the best-recommended route for a new author to get their book and name out there was with the free read option. I went with this. While the book's release and launch was a great success, I wasn't getting review takers. It was all new to me.

But I'd learned, reviews were a key to book sales. I knew the book might not have been what some were expecting; it was full of family, death, spirit, signs, faith, and God. It was also soulful.

I felt it was well written as I was receiving many personal messages. But no review takers. A week later, I purchased the book online to see what a reader saw. Just because; just to see. My heart sunk to the pit of my stomach. My gut knotted, a hot sweat engulfed my body. A feeling of sickness, and paranoia, swept through me.

Some of the captions were off-center. A few pictures weren't lined up, or we're on the next page. After the time-consuming work trying to complete it, it wasn't right! Being a person with an anxious nervousness, OCD traits, and previously a legal assistant, perfection was always warranted. This was far from it.

I was rushed on time in the end. Between the numerous edits, and the uploading of the many photos I had, trying to configure them to Amazon's formatting, I was hustling. After numerous retries and attempts, I thought it was good.

So many nights at the computer, for a deadline that appeared to be destined. There was also the largest factor in; I didn't share the whole story. So, in reality, challenges continued. I needed to fix and correct the errors.

I also wondered if I would ever be able to share the whole story. I had not. I didn't know how to tell or describe what had been presented in appearance in my trashcan.

ORBS, SPIRIT, OR ANGELS

Christmas was upon us. The year seemed to slip away.

Once the boys got older, we exchanged and opened our family Christmas gifts at home. There was no longer the need to take Santa with us to Mom and Dad's for Christmas morning. This year was the same. We opened gifts on the evening of December 23rd and drove the hour drive to Salina the next day.

With Clyde's passing in June, we would celebrate Christmas Eve at my sister Kathy's house. Christmas dinner would be at Mom's on Christmas Day. It would lighten mother's load from hosting both.

The newest, hottest Christmas activity, was an ugly shirt contest. We planned to partake, but not necessarily with a shirt only. Any Christmas attire was acceptable. There were more that participated than not. It was, of course, an option.

We had made-up Santa and reindeer decorated shirts. One particular shirt went as far as having make-believe reindeer poop on it. There was a gift-wrapped walking body. There were lights, balls, and bells attached.

I went to Goodwill looking for ideas. I came across a large white, straw, round billed hat with heart diamond rhinestones around the brim. I also found a glittery styrofoam angel, which was about 6-foot tall. I think they were personally there for me, so I bought them.

Afterward, I went to the local craft store and purchased a large set of angel feathered wings and a single small package of fluffy, white feathers. The large angel wings went on the front of the hat in the center, and the small single feathers were glued on throughout the entire hat. The larger styrofoam angel was attached to the back, standing tall over the top of the hat. It turned out magically. It was, for sure, me! Angels were now a part of my daily life.

This year we were missing two more loved ones. Lenny and Clyde. Their presence, sadly felt. Reminiscing memories of the past were spoken throughout the night. We missed them so much. I was thankful and found comfort in the constant signs. Believing my brothers and other loved ones were never far. It also meant they were with us tonight. It was a true blessing.

A couple of days later, I uploaded the Christmas photos of both gatherings from my phone to the computer. I hadn't looked at any of them yet. Time hadn't allowed it.

On our family Christmases, the question of the night is always, who's passing out the gifts. Who is going to be Santa? This year, nothing had changed. Boys, or should I say, my men, never wanted to pass out gifts. It was always my treat.

Now, as I scrolled through the photos on the computer, it was a photo of myself passing out the gifts, in which I stopped. I had to take a closer look. In the photo, the television screen behind me looked odd. What was on it? Or, better yet, what was in it? It didn't look like a sports show, which would have been on, as the bottom scroll bar suggested.

There were two white, circular spheres on the TV screen—one small, one large. The screen background, I thought, carried the look of old wood planks—the bottom plank looking to be disintegrating or decaying. My mind, or inner voice, says it looks like the inside of an ancient, wooden casket. It decayed after many years of being in the ground.

Discovery was taking me places outside the norm. Here, I wondered in curiosity, could the circular white spheres be orbs? An orb, in researching, is described as a sphere of light energy. They are generally white, but may also vary in colors.

They are circular in size and have been associated with being spiritual beings, light energy, or angels. They are generally captured in photos and can be rare to see with the naked eye.

I later discovered the photo was on live mode, giving a short video of the image. It shows the white spheres are clearly not a light reflection. The scene is 100% a spiritual, mystical phenomenon.

It was back in July when I felt something hovering directly on my right shoulder. There was this dominant feeling, and presence, of something shadowing, lingering upon me. It was somewhat eerie, the feeling. But I was comforted, believing it was an angel. I'd been told previously by the Spiritual Advisor I had three angels very close to me.

I was left to contemplate if this could be a sign, in truth. Showing the closeness and reality of a spiritual energy source. Although it could be angels, I believe it could also be the spirit of my brothers.

Afterward, I headed to my Amazon book page. The book reads and sales had slowed down. I was not promoting it due to what I found when I purchased it a few weeks ago. Corrections were needed. It was hard to expect sales. Therefore, I wasn't checking the site daily, like when the book was first published a month ago.

That day though, after uploading the Christmas photographs to the computer, I checked it. I was surprised when it showed one single sale. The date, Christmas Day. The day we celebrate the birth of Jesus Christ. It took me back to my vision. God was holding my book. He gestured to sit down at the side of my bed to read it.

I take this as another confirming, good sign. Everything was happening in God's light. In ACTS 18:9:

One night the Lord spoke to Paul in a vision: "Do not be afraid; keep on speaking, do not be silent."

It is in these continued incidents, "coincidences" experiences, and occurrences, that allow me to trust in the process and keep on in faith and myself.

ITCHING, SCRATCHING, AND SARAN WRAP

Another year was ending, onto a new one. Awakening brings new vocabulary, senses, and feelings to your existence. The New Year was only days away. I looked forward to it, along with new intentions. I also looked back at what I'd discovered and removed the past year.

As I did a rerun of life, I was taken back, a long way back, to my childhood. I would have been six years old, as I remember it.

I recall the classroom was on the North end, ground level, of the two-storied small Middle School. Close to the cafeteria and restrooms. The most accessible access for the young first-grade students to get to. This goes with my memory of trying to hide the arm wraps. At least, that was the memory held in my mind.

I'd been scratching and itching at my inner forearms. How long I do not recall. The center of my arms, opposite of the elbows, itched. So I scratched. I'd scratch obsessively until they became raw with open sores, blood, and scabs.

Local medical treatment was unsuccessful in diagnosis, treatment, or cure. An outside source was necessary. My parents and I would travel the long three-to-four-hour drive trip to Wichita to see a specialist. It was a never-ending drive, passing through small towns along the way. This in light of seeking advice for me on what had become a health concern.

I recall it being a large, tall, red brick building. The name of the building was called The Brown Building, which was displayed boldly on the front. Inside houses numerous doctors and physicians of specialty types.

After arriving from the long drive, we entered the building and were escorted down a long corridor to a large, oversized, sterile white, painted room. The room was filled with chairs, lined along the four long exterior walls. The chairs were all occupied with children and grown-ups of all ages.

The front desk was a window with a cage-type look. The window in the wall was supported with round steel poles as a protective barrier to the other side. It was frightening to me. Behind the window were nurses and medical personnel. They were adorned in white gowns, white hose, white caps, and white shoes.

The atmosphere was very hospital-like. It was a sterile-looking place. We checked in. The wait was long. It was difficult to sit and be still, wiggling in the chair, scratching at my arms. After what seemed like hours, we were escorted to a small medical room.

The nurse spoke with and questioned my parents. Shortly after that, a doctor, his sterile appearance matching the nurses, appeared in his long white knee-length coat.

After examination and discussions with my parents, a medicated cream was recommended. Instructions for applying were given. It would need to be applied twice daily; once in the morning, and again at bedtime.

Once applied, saran wrap would need to be wrapped around my arms to keep it from being rubbed off. I cannot attest to the diagnosis. It was so long ago. But I believe it was categorized under a nervous condition, anxiety.

It was well known; I wasn't able to sit still. The teachers spoke of it; my parents spoke of it. And well, they would say, "I had ants in my pants!"

In time, with the use of the cream and inability to scratch the area due to the saran wraps, the wounds healed. My thought and attention were taken away from being able to scratch, taking the need and want away from my mind.

It took care of the repetitive nervous action and the compulsive habit of scratching at my forearms. Today's diagnosis would, in my opinion, be an Obsessive-Compulsive Disorder (OCD). The impulsive repetition of an action or behavior due to anxiety, apprehension, nervousness, or fear.

UNTOUCHED PAGES

It was March 2016 when I spoke with a priest at church. I mentioned to him that day that I received Flowers from Heaven after my brother died. When I said it, his eyes lit up. A sparkle, a gleam enlightened them and his face. I stated I'd written a book. I inquired if he would be interested in reading it.

He showed excitement and agreed immediately. He gave me his home email, asking that I send it to him. After a few attempts, it was apparent that a paper copy would be better. A time to meet at his home was scheduled for the next week. Because my story was not yet a paperback edition, I printed off a paper copy.

I arrived on time. It took a short while for him to answer. We entered the house, and I followed him to the living room area, where we both took a seat. He was on the chair. Myself on the couch. He was such a nice Father! He had a cheerful personality and a heartfelt laugh and smile.

He was easy to speak to as we spoke about him, his family, and his life-long devotional work. He inquired about myself and my family; my husband and boys.

We talked about my book, the flowers I received, and some of the happenings and experiences I had. I explained in detail how I'd received the "Flowers from Heaven." He smiled in delight upon hearing it.

I then brought up the chakras. The spiritual energy centers I'd learned about. I questioned if he knew of them. He stated that he had not. He tried to repeat the word. He was struggling with the pronunciation. He and I were both laughing after multiple attempts.

When he agreed to read my book, I was excited. I hoped with his age and years of priesthood, he would be a great historian. I thought he might have been told or heard of other spiritual experiences. I was surprised when he commented he had not.

We ended the evening speaking of current events, masses, and church functions. He was funny, speaking his opinions of things at the church. I left the three-ringed binder, which contained the printed copy of the book inside. He would get back to me when done reading it.

It was two weeks later when I saw him at church. He was the priest for the late mass. I greeted him good morning afterward. Again, I felt his eyes sparkle when he saw me. He stated he was done with the book. He mentioned it didn't do anything for him. I later contacted him to schedule a time to pick the bookbinder up.

When I stopped by his home the next week, he was cooking a rhubarb pie. He had his cooking apron on. An adorable sight to see. This elderly priest, cooking, making a homemade pie. From scratch!

We sat in the two chairs available at the small kitchen table, that was pushed up against the wall in the corner. We chatted as he watched the timer that sat on the table— waiting patiently for it to ring.

We didn't talk about the book. He didn't bring it up, so neither did I. Once the timer rang, and the pie was done, I gestured it was time to go. We rose and entered the living room where the binder sat on his table by the door. He retrieved it, handed it to me, and thanked me.

When I returned home, I looked inside the binder. I noticed the papers placed in the back, inside the pouch of the notebook, appeared to be untouched. I ran out of paper sleeve holders and put the remaining ten pages in the back-cover pocket.

Here it was apparent they had not been removed or read. If so, there would've been some type of creases from being taken out and handled by his old, unstable, aged hands. They appeared untouched, unremoved, and unread.

My mind wondered. Was it his eyes or the story? He spoke of eye problems and his recent doctor's appointments in our emails, and at our first visit. Because he had nothing to say at all, and the pages appeared untouched, I wondered if he didn't read it because he was unable to; or could it have been he started and stopped due to the spirituality, leaving me once again with no answers and no guidance.

It's disheartening; no one seems to have an answer or wants to talk to me about my spiritual experiences. And I am left to ponder, why that is.

COINCIDENCES

With the continued numbers of coincidental happenings bringing me to my present state and continuing to appear, I've come to believe they are guidance. It was my job to interpret them. Death had brought a new form of communication from the other side.

But, how does one confirm the existence of coincidences and synchronicities? To experience situations, and happenings, in a manner in which they correlate to something else. How would one ever determine if it is, or is not, related to something else?

In April 2016, I contacted Dr. Bernard Beitman, founder of Coincidence Studies, via Twitter. He's a Professor and Psychitrist, and renowned author of the book "*Connecting with Coincidence.*" (Dr. Beitman, founder of coincidence studies. https://coincider.com/about-dr-beitman/)

He has edited two issues of Psychiatric Annals that focus on coincidences and has received two national awards for his psychotherapy training program. He was kind enough to respond to me on his Twitter post. We subsequently shared emails back and forth. I forwarded him the transcript of my book and the "Amazing Butterfly Totem Dance" video.

He responded, saying my stories were "reminders of the ever-present mystery surrounding us. The questions your experiences provoke will be helpful to those who encounter them. I like to say, coincidences alert us to the mysterious hiding in plain sight."

He also commented, "the butterfly dance is delightful. Did he/she get tired out at the end?" I explained it was my emotions giving out in the end. Not the butterfly.

With the constant awareness and presence of numbers and signs, I continued to believe I was on a given path. The angel numbers were "text" messages. Their constant presence continued to speak to me. While you can find different definitions of the numbers, called Angel Numbers, many come down to similar theories.

In the number 333, I was protected and guided by the Ascended Masters, the holy trinity. The 555's signified a significant change was coming. The 444's told me my angels were near. The 222's told me to keep my faith and stay positive. Everything was working out.

It was easy for me to keep my thoughts positive. The Universal codes were everywhere and the numbers from the other side were constant, telling me so. As my mother downsized to her Condo, I brought home an alarm clock she no longer needed. I could use it on my side of the bed and eliminate the need to use the one on Al's side.

After plugging it in, I was unable to set the time on it. It wasn't normal. It wasn't moving time, as it should have. Geez, how hard could it be, right? Al was the king of electronics. I would have him set it when he got home from work.

Yet, when he tried, after his few attempts, he too could not get it set at the correct time. The buttons and movements were strange. The time wouldn't move in unison with the numbers correctly, and after a gallant effort, he too gave up. I never unplugged it, nor did I remove it. It stayed on my nightstand.

The clock became an angel clock. Though the time was off, it didn't matter the time of day, nor the hour, when I entered the room or awoke in the night; it routinely showed triple sequenced numbers. It was impeccably crazy. Just ask my husband!

Here, I came to believe the coincidences were the mystical, magical assistance from above, and the Universal Source of Creation. Everything was aligning for a reason, in divine guidance. There were no longer coincidences in life. Everything was happening for a reason.

PRE-EXISTING CONDITION

I loved my fantastic career in the dental field for 20 years. I enjoyed working with the patients and experiencing every aspect of a dental office. I assisted chairside, maintained medical records, monitored medications, took vitals, and assisted in patients' care in surgery, office, and hospital settings. This, along with the anesthesia course I completed, gave me outstanding knowledge into the medical side of health care.

Then there was my experience in the law firm. Working for a worker's compensation and an insurance liability lawyer was an exciting career too. One assignment I did as a legal assistant is that I requested medical records of plaintiffs. I then compiled a chronology of those records onto spreadsheets.

In this, I can assure you, everything you've discussed or been seen for in any medical, health or dental visit, is documented in your patient records. Or should be. Those documents are available to insurance companies, or anyone, under court order.

With this knowledge, I knew, if I chose to speak of my experiences to someone in the medical field, it would be forever etched into my very own medical records. And I wondered what the diagnosis would be? Was there a spiritual awakening diagnosis? Or could it be diagnosed and classified as grief, depression, psychotic, or hallucinations?

My personal experience taught me that an insurance company has the right to deny a person coverage for a medical condition when switching to their new company as an individual. To seek professional answers in my spiritual and not ordinary experiences would mean it would be documented into my chart.

Here, I wondered, could this give a "new" insurance company the right-of-way to deny me eligibility and coverage of psychiatric care, counseling, or therapy if it were needed in the future? My physician and I have spoken briefly about receiving signs on a couple of occasions—both off the record.

My concern comes from personally experiencing the pre-existing condition clause from an insurance company. I'd been denied coverage in the past due to a congenital disability.

I was four or so when I was hospitalized with a kidney infection. IV fluids and antibiotics were being administered. This was done through the thighs of my legs. My tiny, teeny, pencil-shaped thighs; the needles, as I recall, were haunting.

The long, humongous appearance of the pointed metal object was frightening. It appeared the needles would go through my whole leg. It would take all of everyone to hold me down, on the bed, for the insertions.

It was unlike today's IV therapy. The IV's back in those days were placed daily. With fluids and antibiotics injected until the bag was empty. Once the liquid was drained from the hanging IV bag, the needle was removed, rather than keeping in place, as they are done today.

I recall the last day of treatment; after the two previous days and IV placements, I wanted no part of it. I wanted no more! I fought, I cried, and I begged not to have the needles inserted again. I lost, 'one more time', they bartered, 'then you get to go home'. And in the end, they, of course, succeeded.

It was then my parents were told the news by the doctor. They would need to keep an eye on my kidneys. There was a concern in which they needed to be aware of. As time went on, the infections became chronic. The antibiotics, the trips to the doctor, the urine samples, all became routine.

I recall starting my menstrual cycle. I initially believed it was my kidneys bleeding. The lower abdominal and back cramping was normal with the kidney and bladder infections. I hadn't yet experienced the symptoms of the female reproduction cycle to know any different.

Shortly after marriage, we moved to the Panhandle of Oklahoma. Without seeking another physician, I traveled numerous trips back home. It was a four-hour drive. The burning when urinating was back again. The pain in my lower back and right side was there.

Another urine analysis would be taken. Another positive result for infection. More antibiotics and a pill that turns my urine orange. It consumed me. In time, I was placed on a disinfectant medication for the bladder. I would take it daily to assist in keeping my bladder and kidneys clean from bacteria. It did slow down the frequencies, but not enough.

After our move back to Kansas, a year later, my physician recommended diagnostic x-rays. They were scheduled, but not without what I would call "my luck."

The prep directions were given. This consisted of eating nothing but broth or clear liquids for 24 hours beforehand. Everything needed to be cleaned out. It sucked. The day before my appointment, I followed the procedures and prepared myself.

Chicken broth was the choice for lunch and supper. I went to bed before sundown to try and forget the anguish of my growling stomach.

I arrived at the hospital for the x-rays the next morning: paperwork and health questions needed to be answered. As the nurse spoke through the questions, she asked if I was pregnant. I replied, "I don't think so." This would be the wrong answer, as she would question me now.

I stated I was not on the pill but didn't expect I was pregnant; we were taking other precautions. I guess there was always a slight chance. I couldn't say no for sure. It wasn't like we weren't having sex.

After much ado, a blood test was taken. I was sent home for another 24-hours of fasting and no solid foods. The test results would be available the next morning when I returned. I was distraught at the thought of another day without solid food. I was starving. I went home and slept the day away.

The next morning, I was up and again headed to the hospital. The blood test was negative, and the x-rays were completed. But first, I had to go through that extra day of emotional glitch. Nothing ever seemed to go easy for me when it came to my health. I took myself out to breakfast afterward.

It was a Wednesday afternoon. I was off work and was napping when the phone woke me. I rose from the bed and went to answer the phone that hung on the wall in the dining room. It was my doctor, he stated we needed to talk and that I may want to grab a chair.

Half-awake, hearing those words, I walked dazed to the kitchen table and sat down. He stated my x-rays showed my right kidney was not a kidney; it was deformed and extremely small. It looked more like a kidney bean than a kidney. I was most likely born with the defect.

I am in shock, wondering if I am dreaming. Is this conversation real, or will I awake? I want to wake up. Now! The next few months were spent with a multitude of tests and x-rays, with medical appointments that were scheduled in Wichita. That drive three to four hours away. There would be more x-rays with injected dyes.

I was given a gallon-sized container to save my urine over 24 hours. After final testing and results, I was referred to a urologist in Hays. He would do the surgery and remove my deformed kidney: the procedure, a nephrectomy.

I was scared to death. I was twenty-one and having one of my kidneys removed. The other one was enlarged due to overworking for two. I wondered how people lived with one kidney. Later, I learned they/we do.

The surgery went like clockwork. Other than the emotional trauma and the extreme pain in my side from being cut open, I survived. The kidney was removed, and the healing began. I stayed on the antibacterial medication for the next year as a precaution. There were no more infections.

But it came with an expensive life price. With it came a pre-existing condition, strapped to me and my body. In 1988, the oil patch went downhill. We made a move to Manhattan, Kansas, where Al would attend Vo-tech school to learn a new trade.

This also meant he would be unemployed. Because I had not yet found a job that may have medical insurance benefits, we would need to purchase single-family medical insurance coverage on our own.

The applications were completed and signed. The check was written for payment and mailed to the same major insurance company we had prior, with Al's employment. Approximately three weeks later, we received the identification cards in the mail. Along with the cards was a letter reviewing our coverages.

There was a notification of a clause at the bottom of the page, a pre-existing condition clause. It was applied to me regarding my kidneys or lack of. It stated there would be no coverage for treatment related to my kidney and urinary tract.

They were kidding, right? This would be the main reason why I/we needed the medical insurance coverage. After a call to the Company, it became a reality. A defect I was born with now made me a statistic of non-coverage through personal health insurance. How crazy sad was that?

With this, at this time, I'd chosen not to disclose and seek professional medical assistance in this spiritual path. There was no need, not now anyway. My health was doing well. Exceptionally well, in fact. The only thing I needed to do, was figure out the how's, why's, and meaning, of the formed ashes.

APOLOGIZE, RIGHT NOW!

You need to apologize. Right now! Yep, you may have heard it. As a child, you were asked to apologize to your brother or sister for picking or retaliating on them. It was asked of you, and taught, to apologize for being unfair or mean. For taking responsibility for what wasn't kind or appropriate. You were asked to apologize, in forgiveness and penance.

Religions teach forgiveness; parents and teachers teach it. Life teaches it. They are teaching us to be sorry for our wrongful actions. It's a confession of our wrongdoing, it's part of the growing respect in life deal. Confessing our transgressions, sins in forgiveness builds good character and morals. It would also help you get to Heaven.

In religion, we ask for forgiveness for our wrongdoings. Now, I was learning forgiveness was real. In forgiving, one frees themselves, releasing the inner turmoil and blocked energy from the emotions. These are stated to be related to what causes illness in life.

Here, I began forgiving. Forgiving people and events I had endured that left a mark of unhappiness, sadness, judgment, bitterness, or fear, on and in me. I forgave myself for life's choices and situations that were not of good nature. We've all been there, in some way or another.

I found those occurrences and internal memories are hidden in my subconscious that was affecting me emotionally and mentally—affecting my health and my every being. This is where I began to heal. I was releasing the negative experiences and energy.

And as it would be, it appeared, God was testing me. To see how sincere, I was in my forgiveness. For some I was forgiving, those whom I held an inner grudge from past trauma, of unkindness and unfairness, were accepting my friend requests online.

Except, I had not requested their friendship. I had not searched anyone out, clicked on that friendship button wanting to be their online friend. I blamed my husband, stating he hit a wrong button on the iPad, causing the acceptance. He objected, of course.

I was also receiving friend requests from the same. This is where I took it as God wanting to know how serious I was in my forgiveness.

So I accepted their friendship request. Not to be their long lost good friend, but to show I could accept them no matter what pain or heartache they may have caused me. I forgave them, not for them, but for me. I was learning; forgiveness was healing.

Yet, it can be challenging. How do we forgive someone who hurt us in a way we can never forget? Someone who broke our heart and treated us like shit, and took advantage of us, taking our mind, and a piece of it, and our inner being through it.

And, because we say we've forgiven them, does it mean we indeed forgave them? Why would it matter, anyway? No one will ever know if we genuinely forgave or did not forgive someone. Right?

Well, I was learning. Learning, healing the past and forgiving shifts consciousness and body energy. It's not that the incident or event didn't happen. You can't remove the memory, but you can remove the negative energy held inside that emotion. This negative energy is hidden and can be manifesting into the very diseases we carry.

Removing this energy makes way for new life energy, healing energy, bringing along new positive health. With it, we heal our cells, immune system, mind, body, spirit, and soul. My findings told me, if I forgave and apologized internally, to myself and others, along with my ancestors who may be involved as well, for the anxiety and nervousness and disease I carried, it would open new energy. Now within a short period, I, and my health, have transformed.

With my belief of being heavenly guided, along with the introduction of the chakras, and life energy healing, I changed me and my health. I opened a new doorway to life and my physical and mental wellbeing. Through forgiveness, self-affirmations, and quieting my mind, life was turning another direction.

The heart is connected to the soul. All that affects the heart affects the soul. This is where anxiety and depression come in. If we don't remove hurt, heartache, and trauma, the negative energy attaches to us in emotions, wearing on us, causing stress, anxiety, depression, illness, and diseases.

In apologizing and forgiving, it isn't for the other person. It is for us, for our peace and wellbeing. To remove the negative inside is for our own wellbeing. Holding hurt and grudges only deplete our good life force energy.

I forgave myself for being so rigid and judgmental of myself all those years. I was the way I was. The way I was born and raised. Just like all of us. Forgiveness was forgiving my ancestors as well; those who may have put their diseases, habits, addictions, and poverty on me through the family tree.

Research and science written say we carry attachments in our DNA, and ancestry; genetics. The high blood pressure, cancer genes, diabetes, mental psyche, body, and spirit. All in our heredity chemistry. Here, I found myself forgiving my ancestors for what they may have to do with me, my health, and my life.

I found it was my chance to let it all out. To make peace with those who'd taken advantage of me somehow, in the way they treated me. To make peace with me. All the things that we, as humans, go through in life, on any given day, needed the energy released.

The siblings, girlfriends, boyfriends, bosses, coworkers, and family-it was refreshing, uplifting, and rewarding. I was saying good riddance to multiple two-faced people's actions, lies, and memories that passed through life.

You know, it's something no one thinks about. At least I never did. If someone treated me like crap, it was part of life. It was nothing I could control. I always believed Karma knew the truth. What we reap is what we sow. God knew the truth. That's what mattered.

Now, I knew I hadn't forgiven, freely, some experiences. I still held some inner grudges. It's human nature. But I found, if we don't let the experience go in forgiveness, it doesn't remove that deep, inner, replay film. With a button always being pushed and triggered. The memory silently weighing on our human self and wellbeing.

As I sat out back, in the quiet of nature, the forgiving began. Everyone, including me, myself, and I, which affected me sadly or negatively, was being let go. I forgave myself for allowing people to treat me, as they may have.

The people whose hormones, ego's, popularity contests, and self-loathing controllers who took advantage of me; you know how it goes. You've possibly been there, through it, too. Then, it was what it was. It still is. I couldn't, or can't, do a thing about how people are.

In my efforts, it was removing the lower energy trapped inside my body and cells. It was energizing me and my whole being. It was working on what I was doing. My confidence, self-esteem, and my inner-self woke to new energy. I was aligning with myself in writing and gave the resources to share my journey.

Through it all, I found an inner peace, which I now know, could only come from my inner-self. No medication, as I will attest to, would be successful. My simple to do forgiveness, releasement, sun energy, baths, crystals, oils, meditations, breathing techniques, and the 'I AM' affirmations had me detoxed and recharged with new energy and rhythm flow, outlook, and health.

In forgiveness, it allowed me to open a new awareness and energy within me. It opened me up from an inner infection of disease to love, in myself, for others, and all things.

"Lord, how many times shall I forgive my brother or sister who sins against me? Up to 7 times? Jesus answered, I do not say to you up to seven times, but up to 70 x 7." Matthew 18:21-22

PARTIES, MEMORIES & MUSIC

Chris was turning 30! His birthday was Saturday, April 21st, and he was throwing a birthday party bash! It was to be a hog roast, with a live band. He told his dad he needed to outdo his 40th birthday party in which we roasted a hog, had a live band, and a backyard and house full of people.

This was something we did a few times, holding family reunions as well. There was enough family, extended family, and friends, to enjoy great weekend gatherings. These were events Lenny loved to say he couldn't come home, but arrangements were being made.

It was usually a week or two before the party; we would get the call. Lenny had previously told everyone he couldn't get off work, again. Yet, he was calling with flight arrangements. He and the family would be here. Mum's the word. It would be a surprise. The flight times were given, and Al would be there to pick them up in Kansas City.

And as he planned it, it was always a wonderful surprise. That was him! The weekends would include horseshoes, kid's baseball games, and golf tournaments. There was eating and drinking and live music, all in the name of making memories. Lots and lots of beautiful memories.

Now, 20 years later, Chris is taking after his dad. He was throwing the party! Like they say, "like father, like son." He didn't fall far from the tree. I went to Walmart on that Friday. I picked up the cupcakes I previously ordered, as well as a few other last-minute items. Once I had everything I needed, I worked my way to the registers and got in line.

A woman is in line in front of me. We made small talk as we waited patiently for our turn in line. Standing there, I noticed something sticking out the back of her jean pocket. My mind quickly says it looks like a wing. I wondered to myself if it was a butterfly wing.

The longer we stood there, the more I itched to ask her what it was in her back jean pocket. Yet, I didn't. I pondered if it might be a sign. And now, she has moved forward and is unloading her cart onto the conveyor belt. I patiently waited. When she was done, she paid and moved on.

I'd placed my few items on the conveyor belt. The cashier is running my things through as I noticed the woman who was before me had stopped at the empty cash register island in front of us. She was frantically searching through her purse, emptying the contents out on the checkout conveyor.

As I watched her, I could only think it might be her car keys she was looking for, which could be what's in her back pocket. I leave my check out and walk her way.

I questioned if she was looking for her keys. "Yes, yes, I am," she said. I told her I thought they were in her back pocket. At that moment, the feelings and the eye contact we shared were of mystical wonderment. She is thinking, how do you know? And I am thinking, I know, and I want to see them.

She reached back behind her and pulled the keys out of her back pocket. She let out a sigh of relief. It is now I get to see what is in her back pocket that was sticking out. The keyring she held displayed an angel. "Dang," I said out loud.

I told her I'd noticed them sticking out of her back pocket as we stood in line. I said I believed it to be a butterfly wing sticking out. I didn't think of an angel. She proceeded in telling me the angel was in memory of her son. He'd passed not long ago.

Now, I told her I believed it was a sign for me; that I received messages and signs from my brothers who passed away. Again, our eyes met; a wave of awe fell upon her face. She told me she believes she receives signs from her son as well.

He was an avid Bald Eagle lover. Since his passing, Eagles have appeared frequently. They were forever in her path. I confirmed to her; I believed they were indeed signs. I told her about my published book. She appeared excited and stated she would be looking for it.

I returned to my checkout and paid. As I left walking towards the exit, I wondered what the odds were. The odds I would be in line, at that moment, to help find her angel keys and to share our experiences of signs from our loved ones.

Chris and friends were up early the next morning. They prepped and prepared the hog for the Cajun Microwave Hog Cooker. It consists of a large stainless steel box with a decorative wooden exterior. The steel top cover is used for coals, cooking from the top, rather than the bottom. It's on wheels and is portable. They purchased it together a few months back.

They iced beers and refreshments, set up tables and chairs, and then the wait was on. It was going to be a beautiful day. No wind was expected, and the high-temperature was to be in the 60s. Perfect weather!

The party was taking place at a friend's house. In 1988, when we moved to Manhattan, our newest neighbor became a good, life-long friend. The party was being held at his residence. He lives outside of town, with a perfect country setting.

The house was set back in, off the main road. The front faces West, of the South running roadway. There is a detached, 2 1/2 car, older garage, that sits off to the West of the house. Behind the house, on the Eastside, is a dirt road. It is somewhat hidden with trees, and if you'd not been there before, you may pass it up.

The dirt road takes you down to a lower ground level. Here you find a charming country setting. Large trees cover the grounds, with newly growing leaves budding through. There was a small stage and another garage type storage building. A large limestone rock fire pit sits between the building, and the wooded area, where the hog was cooking.

There is roughly a 24-foot drop behind the upper detached garage, which is visible from down below. The landscaped hill has limestone rock, trees, and new grass, flowers, and spring, coming through.

Off towards the lower driveway entrance was a handmade stairway. It spirals up the hill, bringing you to the rear of the house. It's made of flat limestone rocks. The rocks are somewhat out of alignment due to age, use, and ground movement. One must be careful and watch their step.

Friends and family began arriving around two and continuing throughout the afternoon and evening. The day started down below where the hog was cooking. Beers were consumed as the pig cooked. Friends were mingling, catching up, and enjoying the beautiful day as the music blared from the massive oversized speakers by the storage building.

Time went fast. It was 4:30 p.m. already, and dinner would be ready at 5:00 p.m. I walked the limestone steps up to the house, and the detached garage, to set out the side foods. Reaching the top of the steps, I first headed towards the house, to use the inside restroom and wash up.

Approaching the three wooden steps leading to the house's porch, I see a rock lying directly in the middle center wooden step. It's small and limestone, the shape, a heart. I picked it up, admiring and loving it. I thanked my loved ones for letting me know they were with us today, in spirit. I put it in my front jean pants pocket.

The hog was wheeled up shortly thereafter, and dinner was served. The buffet line formed fast. Within an hour, everyone had been through the line. The music would begin soon.

I hadn't heard the news until earlier in the day. Two bands were playing. One to play shortly after dinner, and one to play late into the evening. This is where Chris did outdo his dad. Two bands in one night was a first.

The stage was set up inside the upper-level double car garage. Our friend, and host, is a musician who plays the drums. His band is playing first, and the second band, who are his friends, will play after his.

I had a new rhythm with my awakening and energy healing—a new vibrational swag and beat, per se. Music was a part of my daily therapy.

Now, with the bands and the music, I had the vibes and danced. I danced the night away! From the time the first classic rock music started, I danced until the end of the night. I danced with my boys and Al. I danced with my mother, sisters, and friends. I even danced with many of the boys' friends.

Life was suddenly carefree. I was enjoying my new freedom and the moment. It'd become apparent in removing the unwanted brain fog and lower energy; I removed the weights that kept me from fully feeling my life rhythm.

Music is said to have a spiritual connection to the soul. It's known to be the go-between from the spiritual world and life. Spirit speaks to us through music and songs. They have no voice, so they use any way of getting a message to us, including music, lyrics, and songs. The radio, speaker, and music were continually speaking to me.

It's when you've got them on your mind, and you climb in the vehicle, and "I will always love you," starts to play. Or you hear their favorite song, in the synchronicity of a memory. It's your loved one's message.

The portable speaker we went back into the store and purchased for ourselves became my daily therapy. Music is noted to be as good as Yoga. It also carries vibrations. Which I am learning a lot about.

A Harvard Medical Study stated music therapy is a burgeoning field. A music therapist, treating with music, can evoke emotional responses to relax or stimulate people to heal. A growing list of research attests that music therapy is more than listening to your favorite song.

It can improve your quality of life, reduce anxiety, help with speech loss, cancer therapy, pain relief, and improve the quality of life for dementia patients.

Music puts out vibrations that pulsate through the body. These vibrations and tones can change the energy in your body, reducing stress and anxiety. This is known to impact your physical wellbeing, as well as your emotional wellbeing. Releasing tension and energy and promoting emotional balance within the body.

Healing with sound dates back to ancient Greece when it was used in an attempt to cure mental disorders. Singing and humming certain sounds are healing as well. The vibrations, and tones, can balance the chakras. Besides all this, what an enjoyable, fun, freeing way to heal.

STALKERS

We left this morning for Scottsdale, Arizona. Al has professional training that was beginning June 6th. Rather than fly and go by himself, I joined him. We were taking two extra vacation days, coming home through Colorado and the mountains.

En route, heading West on I-70, I reached for my phone in my purse to check the time. It was 11:11 a.m. (no clock on the stereo in the truck). We both smiled. Right on time, it appeared!

Our first stop on our drive is my hometown of La Crosse. We'd brought with us decorations to place on the graves of family members. We had flowers, artificial birds, and butterflies. We added additional solar lights to each tombstone that had an open slot. When all were decorated, I grabbed my phone for photos to text to the family: the time, 12:22 p.m.

The next stop was Al's hometown of Ness City. Here we had lunch with a friend at a favorite hometown place to eat. It's a little diner, locally owned, and run by our friend's sister, a friend of ours as well.

We arrived coming in on the road that goes East and West through town. The restaurant was on this road. As we approached, a vacant parking spot was open and we pulled in. Across the street was a local tavern.

Exiting the vehicle, I glanced across towards the bar. One lone pickup is parked in front. The rear license plate has the numbers 333. As Al as my forever witness, the angel numbers are constant. It appears they are traveling with us.

Lunch was delicious, as always. Afterward, we visited the cemetery where Al's family is laid to rest. We don't make it back home much anymore, so when we do, we do try to stop.

Now we are again on the road. The final destination for the day is Tyrone, Oklahoma. Three hours away. We would spend the night with friends before heading for Gallup, New Mexico, the next morning.

We exited off the main two-lane highway. After a couple of miles on dirt roads, we turned around, heading back towards the main highway. It appeared this was not the route we should be on. It took a phone call for additional directions.

The dirt roads, with single alphabet letters, were a sign of small-time country living. It took only one set of alphabet letters to cover all the area farm homesteads. It is, out in the boondocks.

We arrived at our destination late afternoon-a bungalow-type farmhouse in the country. The afternoon was spent on the open wood deck, which wraps around two sides of the house. It's a beautiful calm setting. The continuous incoming of birds at the feeders was therapy.

Supper was planned for here as well. Steaks were being grilled, and the outdoor table was set. The evening was spent there talking about old memories and making new ones. There was also a jug of homemade moonshine floating around the table. I personally didn't care for it. But that didn't keep it from getting drunk.

Nighttime had now fallen. It was quiet. Darkness was everywhere. No lights from a city could be seen. The nighttime sky was the tapestry. It reaped millions of stars, a picturesque view you see in the movies of a flawless sky, showing its gloriousness. It was exceptional and captivating.

I found myself yelling out loud to the universe and sky. "Hello," I yelled. Al and I were both taken in by the magnificent beauty. A motion-picture screen, the tiny sparkling lights upon the darkness of the pitch-black screen, had us captured.

While we could've stayed out there forever in the universe's wondrous tapestry, it was now half-past one. It'd been a long day. Tomorrow will be long as well. I hated to go in, it was free out there, but it was time for some shut-eye.

We hit Gallup, New Mexico around five the next day. It was a good seven to eight-hour drive. The drive was uneventful except for loads of truckers on I-40, or US Hwy 66; "Route 66." It's a gateway for truckers hauling freight loads.

One of my biggest fears came in a car. Don't know why it was there. I was a great invisible second brake person. As a passenger, with a car merging onto a highway next to us or a passing trucker, you may find my feet hit the invisible brake on the passenger floorboard.

As a passenger, when someone drove too close to the rear of the vehicle in front of us, my feet may hit the invisible brake, or, maybe, the glove box dash. Driving along the mountainside edge, I may hide my head or close my eyes. It was a fear of unknown circumstances. Medications helped, somewhat.

That day though, I didn't take my prescription anxiety medicine I have available for travel and sleeping. I haven't needed it as much as of late. My new mindset, in faith and belief, told me I was protected; God and the angels were always near. They've been showing me.

It helped to put my fears aside. If something was to happen, it would happen. I could not control situations out of my control. If it wasn't to be, it wouldn't be. I was protected. I was in God's hands.

Otherwise, the weather was sunny. We had good tunes and music, and the miles seemed to travel by fast. After checking in the hotel we had reservations for, we changed clothes and headed for the hot tub and pool area.

The swimming pool was occupied by a family of four; two adults and two small children. The hot tub was empty, which is what we desired. We made a dash to it and spent the next hour, soaking our bodies. It was the perfect therapy and relaxation from two days on the road in the truck.

Dinner consisted of walking to a nearby café. We didn't wander far as the hot tub put us in a melted state. All we needed was something in our tummies before ending our day.

Returning to the Hotel thereafter, we found ourselves in our lounge clothes, and bed, where we drifted off to sleep. The television left on, which is rare for us.

We arose at dawn the next morning. Ready to reach our final destination. Needing to gas up before hitting the road, we pull into the convenient gas station next to the Hotel. Gas pumps are on both sides of the building.

Driving into the lot, the pumps on the west side of the building are full of vehicles pumping gas. Al drives towards a pump to wait in line as I tell him there are more pumps on the other side of the building. I saw them when we pulled in. He reverts and drives towards the other side.

A pump is open, and he pulls in. A vehicle was at the pump directly in front of us. Another is at the pump directly across from them. This vehicle is a van, which is clearly in my view. As I look from my passenger's seat through the front windshield, I am *captured* by what I see.

The vehicle has seat covers on the seats. They display butterflies. Two very large, purple and pink butterflies. One on each seat.

The butterfly is a spiritual sign of transformation and resurrection. As the caterpillar turns into the cocoon, appearing dead, living in darkness, it later transforms into a beautiful winged butterfly. This shows, as humans, we too may transform from the darkness into beautiful human creations.

This, for me, was another sign the angels continued to travel with us. We were guided over to this side of the building for a reason; here it is, to see the butterflies. And I loved it and the angels.

Being right next to the Interstate, it was easy to get back on our route. We traveled for a few hours before pulling off in Flagstaff, Arizona, to eat lunch. There were multiple choices of fast foods, as we decided on one. It felt good to stop and take a break, stretching our legs. Once done, we exit the restaurant. Here another license plate number is in our direct view walking out the door. The number is 333.

The next planned stop before hitting our final destination is Winslow, Arizona. A small, unpopulated town, known for the home of "Standing on a Corner" and "Take it easy," a tribute to Jackson Brown and Glen Frey.

In our family, it is well known Al's favorite song is "Take it Easy." It is "his" song. It was also Lenny's goodbye message. So, when we arrived there, in Winslow, Arizona, we found ourselves standing on the corner of the popular icon setting. It was awesome and yet, bitter-sweet.

We hit the little shops in the direct area around the corner Tribute. We loaded up on photos, t-shirts, and memorabilia.

The tribute brings tourists from all over the world to their tiny little town. After our sightseeing, we returned to our vehicle. Ready for our final destination. The conference, and Scottsdale, Arizona.

Al spends his days in classes, workshops, and seminars. I take the time to myself. I am a tag along for the R&R. He would be here, no matter what. I take the pleasure of accompanying him. Sleeping in, no time schedule, and an excellent book to read. Perfect. There is also pool time.

It's hot as crap in Arizona in the summer. You either stay in, or you need water close by. I'd meet up with other spouses—some with kids. We would spend time together, swim, shop, and have lunch.

But, as we know, time flies! It was a great few days and lots of fun in the hot sun for me, but I was ready to head to cooler weather in Colorado. While it is a different hotness then in Kansas, without the humidity, it was downright scorching hot in Arizona.

Mountains, as I said, were never my friend. My anxiety and paranoia of driving off the cliff, well, it was there. Fear of heights and flying were on the list as well. More drugs.

It was the second trip to Vegas, after the first trip, that I became friends with Dramamine. I took it to help calm me when flying. It did help. Later I switched to prescription anxiety medication.

The first time a family group of us flew to Vegas to see Lenny, a lady behind us on the airplane wanted to give me her drugs to relax me. I didn't take them but learned a lesson for the next time. I was a paranoid freak. I needed my feet on the ground. I needed control. I had neither when I traveled.

I can't recall the last time we drove from one side of the Colorado mountains to the other. It would've been one of the Vegas trips to see Lenny. We'd travel all night to get back home; after 3 to 4 days of casinos, nightlife, and fun.

We would long for our bed, our pillow, and sleep. We would push the all-night drive home. But it was brutal, and not too wise. We did this twice.

Now we prepare to travel more miles down the highways. Through the mountains. The high that day in Scottsdale was predicted to be 110 degrees. Dressed in shorts and flip flops, we are loaded and on the road. It's a good five-hour drive to our motel in Durango.

The scenery, the snow-topped mountains, and the landscape, and clouds. Wow! Was it always this beautiful? Was it always so magical? The valleys and trails. The trees in the mountains. The streams, and the winding, winding roads. The mountain tops covered in snow. The beauty of the land and nature. How did I not see it before?

The clouds hung low in the sky. I shot tons of photos on our route. As we drove, I scrolled back through them. I found a photo in which the clouds looked to be of a young boy—sitting in the clouds. It was spectacular.

The Hotel was tucked back in the lot and was difficult to see from the road as the sun was setting lower. It wasn't an upscale hotel like we just came from. It didn't have a pool, gym, or restaurant. It was a simple, quiet little place with a room to sleep.

It was a U-shaped older building with 15 rooms, all ground level. It would work for the night. When we exited the vehicle to check-in, I was shocked. The temperature was 40 degrees. My shorts and flip flops were no longer adequate. It was downright cold.

Our evening was spent walking the tourist area, the shops, and downtown. A train ride is available through the mountains, which the town was famous for. It had already departed for the day. In our walk, we came upon the notorious old-timer photograph store—the one where you dress up in frontier clothes to have your photo taken.

Al and I did this on our honeymoon. Our 35th wedding anniversary was coming up in July. I want to see if I can get him to do it again, for our anniversary. As we were approaching, I told him we should do it. Dress up, and have our pictures taken. "For our anniversary," I said. "Like we did on our honeymoon."

He responded, "Make it quick." I looked at him, questioning if I'd heard him correctly. Was that a yes? The front door to the store was open to the outdoors. We walked inside. The young gal standing behind the counter was smiling as we walked in. She heard our conversation. As we approached the counter, she leaned over and whispered to me, saying, "Man, he was easy." "Yes," I said, laughing. Yes, he was.

It was a hoot. We laughed. We posed. We were in the moment, having fun, enjoying life, and each other. While it brought memories of 35 years ago, this was more intimate, more personal, than our honeymoon moment. Our love and journey had us growing together.

The clerk helping us made it special. She picked out our clothes and setting from what we described was the scene from our honeymoon. She had us move this way, and that way, as we laughed throughout. We walked out with three 8x10's. We loved them all.

There was this sense of completeness and love of our 35 years together. We ended the evening with dinner in a small yet long, narrow bar. A musician was playing his guitar, singing, and entertaining the crowd in the back area. It was a perfect ending, a perfect day, and evening!

We arrived in Silverthorne, Colorado, at our Hotel, mid-afternoon the next day. We parked in the Hotel lot and walked to the entrance. The car in the check-in driveway of the entrance has a 777 tag. I pointed it out. We both laugh as Al laughingly states, "They are stalking us."

After checking in and showering, we are back out in our vehicle and ready to tour the town. We found ourselves at Dillon Reservoir Lake. It was stunning, serene. The mountains with the snow in the background were breathtaking. The water, a true blue and sparkling clear, it was a true treat to the beauty of mother nature.

We spent an hour walking around the lake, taking in the beautiful view. When leaving, as Al is backing the truck out, I continue to admire the view from the vehicle. Looking backward, I see a car parked in the lot. The tag is 777. It is not the same vehicle that we saw at the motel. Although Al was insisting it was.

Frisco was nearby. We stopped and walked the mile-long streets. We were checking out the souvenir stores. I'd wanted a dream catcher. I'm still not remembering my dreams, but I believe I have them. I continue to wake at night. Sweat pouring out of my body. And I continue to wonder if it is from anxiety in dreams or hormonal.

As we walked, we came to a small shop. In the window is a medium-sized, green feathered, dream catcher. I liked it and had to go in. Al waited outside. I found a rack full where many colors are displayed, but I chose the green one. It was only five dollars. What a bargain!

Hunger was setting in. It was after 5:00 p.m. Nothing on the main street interested us. We returned to our vehicle and drove around the city, looking for other options. We came upon a restaurant off the main road. The parking lot was full. By the looks, it was the place to eat.

We pulled in, finding one lone parking spot available. On the walk towards the entrance, another vehicle license plate is in our path. Again, the 777 number. Al says it's the same vehicle that was at the lake. I don't think it is.

That was a silver van; this is a car. I don't know if it's the car that was at the motel. There've been so many vehicles and numbers; I'm losing track.

We didn't have to wait long to be seated for as busy as the restaurant was. We were taken to a quiet table in a corner. We both ordered the chicken fried steak, which came in a bowl. The chicken fry was served on top of potatoes and gravy. Homegrown green beans with bacon were on the side.

We both must have been starving as we scarfed it down. During dinner, the continuance of seeing the numbers was a part of our conversation. They couldn't all be coincidences. They had appeared our entire journey. Al says they are stalkers.

When done, we returned to the motel, stuffed. We arrived and again, parked in the hotel parking lot. Sitting directly in the row in front of us is another car that holds more numbers. These numbers were 666. We both see it at the same time. I chuckled.

Al immediately stated, "that's bad news." I laughed out loud. I told him only if he thought it was bad; it would be negative. The 666 number in spirituality can tell us to keep our thoughts positive. To stay grounded and balanced in the present moment.

We took the elevator, directly to the left of the front entrance, to our room on the second floor. Once there I hit the light switch to turn on the lights. It's not dark out yet, but the sun was going lower in the sky.

The lights do not come on. I don't believe it's a problem; maybe they're not on that switch. I walk to the table lamp next to the bed, turning the light switch on. No lights. That's strange. I found the television remote and tried the TV. No TV either, now it was obvious, we had no electricity or lights.

I phoned the front desk. The clerk stated some of the lights in part of the building were out. They were working on it. It shouldn't take long. Rather than sit in the room with no electricity, TV, or sound, I tell Al I'm running downstairs to see what's up.

I take the stairs this time. I didn't trust the elevator, which we had just taken to the second floor. As I reached the bottom, I entered directly into the lobby. Some lights were on, but as I took a few steps in, the rest of them in the room, and building, went out. People are now congregating in the lobby.

An elderly gentleman was there with a group of four. He was standing at the check-in counter. Irate at the clerk and the electricity problem. He was loud and causing a scene. He threw his room keys across the counter at the clerk.

At that point, I exited the front door. He was rude. The kid had no control over the situation and what was happening with the lights. I sat outside the front entrance speaking with another guest who chose to accept the lack of electricity outdoors as well.

The gentleman and his group came walking out shortly thereafter, their luggage in hand. I assumed he was given a refund and was headed elsewhere. I don't know if they chose to leave, or if asked to leave. I preferred the latter.

It didn't take long for Al to come down from the room and join us. We sat out front of the motel, with a few other guests that had gathered. It was roughly 30 minutes before the electricity was back on, and we returned inside to our rooms. But in curiosity, I wondered if the 666 may have had a significance in the ordeal, identifying the turmoil ahead, and to stay grounded in the episode. The main thing now was, all was well.

Tomorrow would be another long day. We will arise early again, anxiously making more miles down the highway. This time, for home, seven hours away. It'd been a fabulous trip. We saw lots of beautiful countryside and friends. And we got to share our love, together.

How grateful I was. Grateful to be guided by the "stalkers," as Al would call them. The aligning angel signs and numbers, in their distinguished presence in our travels, no matter what you call it, gave way for me to stay calm and enjoy the travels. It was pure bliss.

A NEW LANGUAGE

It's astonishing, fascinating, and capturing how the numbers are constant in our path. I laugh at Al when he makes fun of them. I tell him it's the angels and the universe's language. It is unconscious how they do appear in the timely manner they do. How does that happen?

I am learning through constant awareness. The synchronicity of the numbers and the overwhelming presence allows me to believe in them, and to decipher them. Spirituality tells us it's the universe, winking at us. So we may stop, look, and pay attention.

The numbers appear as you awaken. Your angels, and spirit guides, guide you, taking your attention to them. Letting you know, it's more than a coincidence. Consciously you become aware of the vibrational language of numbers.

It was the 333 number catching my attention, accelerating my journey with numbers. In scripture, we find Jeremiah 33:3 which states, "Call to me and I will tell you great and unsearchable things that you do not know." Here, I am taken to believe how true this has become.

Numbers are revealed throughout scriptures. Each with symbolism throughout the Bible. These numbers, placed by God, have their own scripture and messages. The numbers, and connections to scriptures, are with merit and meaning.

An article on BibleStudy.org speaks of the meaning of numbers in the Bible. Here it states, "An essential key to understanding the design of God's Word is through the meaning of Biblical numbers. When we search them out and understand them, the connections and patterns of numbers reveal the handiwork of God.

"Although the arrangement of some is apparent, others require research. These patterns found do not exist by random chance but by design. Each one has a particular symbolism attached to it by our Creator."

As I was awakening and led deeper into faith and the numbers, it brought light to numerology. In the study of numbers, you may find answers to life's emotional, mental, and spiritual aspects. Numbers carry vibration along with letters, music, and all creations.

Our birthdate, and name, are attached to us in which life's missions are created. Our time-stamped date of birth aligns with our life destination—the vibration of them, combined for our life path. Hence, you have a horoscope.

Here one becomes captivated as to how intertwined life is. In the cosmic atmosphere, one says numbers carry vibrations, influenced by the solar system. When we look to the solar system, we are taken to the Star of Bethlehem and Three Wise Men, who followed Bethlehem's star. To meet the newborn king. Now we have astrology. All intertwined into Biblical numerology, meanings, and interpretations.

35TH ANNIVERSARY EARTH ANGEL

It was here, July 11, 2016. Our 35th wedding anniversary. It was hard to believe. Time had flown furiously by. With raising the boys, working, and life's responsibilities, here we were. Married for ages and soul mates.

I checked the mailbox at the curb when I got home from work. Mom sent a beautiful anniversary card. Besides the heartfelt saying, it had glittery butterflies on the front. She knows me well. I do love her!

There was also a card addressed to Al only, and I took the liberties to open it. We are one together. It was a thank you card. On the front was a heart made with hands, along with the company's name that sent it. There was also a written message that said, "much more than medicine."

Here, I believe the card is an anniversary wish from the other side. The heart formed out of hands, is a beautiful sign of love. It is a special day for us, and my loved ones love to send cards with messages. I'm taking it.

Besides the love it shows with the heart hands, I believe it also carries a message about the chakras. Through my experience, I believe the simple energy healing I've been doing to be "much more than medicine." Exactly what the cards message said.

Energy healing brings a freedom from negative, low vibe energy of judgment, and self-doubt, compiled from years of mental programming and trauma; it's a reprieve from the daily mental infliction from the rolling mind.

If you follow an energy healing path, you may heal your body, mind, and spirit. Science speaks of Human Energy Fields and Etheric Bodies. That all materials in the physical world are energy. Everything in the universe is made up of energy vibrating at different frequencies.

This, I am finding, is better than medicine; simple techniques, to raise your vibration, or vibes, eliminating diseases and medications, and support in natural, alternative, holistic healing. That is what the card was telling me. To me, it's beautiful!

As it was our anniversary, we were headed out to dinner in celebration. The question now was where were we going. We go over our possibilities as we drive into town. We opted for our favorite steak place.

The wait was short before being escorted to a booth in the middle section of the restaurant. Our waiter is a young African American, meant for us. Throughout dinner, he inquired about us, and we about him.

He was friendly, pleasant, and easy to talk to. He stated he was only here in town for two weeks. He was from Las Vegas. Ha! When that came out of his mouth, those words had Al, and I, instantly looked at each other, making eye contact.

Our minds both internally stated, "Yes! Of course, he was." He said he previously lived here but now lived in Las Vegas. He was back in town to make some money before starting school in the Police Academy, which was in a few months. He was becoming a police officer.

Again, Al and I made eye contact, this time with concern on our minds and faces. With the number of officers killed in the line of duty today, it was with heavy hearts when he spoke of it. Life as an officer today is scary. He was such a nice guy!

He could sense our emotions in our faces. Or maybe it was the vibes (vibrations). He continued by reassuring us it takes good guys to catch the bad guys. By the end of dinner, we felt better about his courage to serve and protect.

When we paid him for the bill, I also gave him a card for my book. I told him when his mind got confused with the meaningless acts of violence he would endure; it may help. It contained faith and a healing of the mind process. He was amazed, accepting with gratitude.

Here, once again, we found ourselves placed where we were supposed to be. At the exact place, for a special meaning and message. I mean, how do you end up with a waiter from your deceased brother's hometown, when you are celebrating your special anniversary day?

There was no doubt it was a sign from my brother Lenny, from Las Vegas. He was letting us know he was with us; wishing us a Happy Anniversary. The waiter, on this day, was an earth angel.

PLAYING THE ODDS

My discovery never stops. I continued to keep playing, playing the odds. The odds I would find a how, on how the totem of souls appeared. The reason, and it's meaning.

It was in August 2016 when I came across an afterlife expert on twitter. I sent the television photos of the orbs/angels via twitter, with hopes he would comment, and he did. He questioned if the orbs were the afterlife of "so and so" (for book purposes). I responded with some BS comment acting like I knew who he was speaking of. I did not.

Since I now have him in conversation, I ask if I can email him some additional photos to look at, i.e., the trashcan photos. Again, he responded, and I emailed him.

I didn't hear back regarding the other photos. A couple weeks later, I sent a reminder. I received a response from his assistant stating he thought he was the wrong person to contact. He didn't believe in this sort of thing. He recommended a paranormal investigator instead.

In my email, I previously asked him if he knew how the form appeared, and if the faces I saw in it, could be related to reincarnation or a past life.

A HOME VISIT

In my online search for people to share my experiences with and possible answers, I found a Body Mind Spirit Directory for Kansas. The directory contained holistic healers, alternative healthcare providers, chiropractors, massage therapists, health food stores, yoga teachers, etc. It was here I found a Spirit, Mind and Body Fair scheduled in Manhattan in August. I saved the site.

As I looked through the vendors listed for the fair, I found some local names of people. My intuition, gut feeling, and spirit guides continued to keep me searching for including the trashcan in my book.

My inner self tells me it is to be shared. It's so amazing, so surreal. I've yet to find anything like it. I feel it's got to be shown. Without it in the story, the entire journey is incomplete.

I put together an e-mail, sending it out to a couple of people on the directory roster who lived in this area. I explained I had written a book, the unknown of the trashcan, and looked for guidance.

I could go back to the original Spiritual Advisor, but I'm looking more for someone to share, without a fee, to get to know on a personal side, someone who understands spirit life, a spiritual friend. Today I received an email response from Amanda.

She was listed in the fair program as a card reader, along with mediumship. She was interested in meeting, but also wanted to know what it was I was looking for. We exchanged a few more emails and voicemails and set a time for her to come to the house on Saturday, five days away.

So I needed to break the news to Al. Being it was a Saturday, he will not be working. Somehow, I don't think I want him around for this visit, nor do I think he would like to be here. I am not sure what to expect.

As I was preparing dinner tonight, I mentioned I had someone coming to the house to visit. I told him he might want to go to Chris' house while she was here. He knew I had been looking, or continuing to search, for answers.

His first comment was, "I hope they don't have an advertisement on their vehicle." Jokingly, I'd mentioned in the past having someone come to the house to see if they could recognize spirit. I think Al has the vision of a Ghostbusters vehicle showing up. Oh, my goodness!

Saturday was getting closer. Friday, I told Al he honestly didn't need to leave if he didn't want to. He said he would see. On Saturday, he decided he would mow the lawn and stay clear of the house while she was here.

Amanda arrived on time. I saw her out the front door as she pulled up in the cul-de-sac. She was driving a dark SUV vehicle. I laughed out loud when I saw it. On her back-side quarter panels, on both sides of her vehicle, were advertisement signs of her spiritual practice. Al was on the mower, and I knew it was only a matter of time before he saw it.

She was taller than me, slender, with long dark hair, pulled back in a ponytail. She carried the look of a cowgirl to me. I invited her in, leading her to the living room and couch. I have my book on hand. In first talking, she was looking for someone who knew of the spirit world as well. She spoke of some of her experiences and judgment that comes with it.

We went through my book. I showed her photos, explaining some of the experiences. She mentioned she continued to have a dream of her painting a picture. She was unsure of the meaning. As we sat there, she took a black heart-shaped Tourmaline stone out of her pocket. She carried it with her. I loved it. I had not yet seen a heart-shaped stone. I would be looking for one for myself.

It is now I mention the trash can, which was in the office. We made our way there. As she entered the room, she stopped in the doorway. On a small desk, I have my memorabilia and my Signs for my Soul book on display.

I'm not sure if she was amazed at what she saw, or the energy she experienced in the room, but I could sense her emotions through her body language and facial expression. The desk's top is covered from side to side with cards, rocks, hearts, feathers, papers, and receipts. It also has an angel candle.

My first book "Signs for my Soul" is displayed, as well as a live plant. The plant I've had since Jamie's funeral, 20 some years ago. It's been re-rooted and transplanted multiple times, and is still a piece of his memory, and continues to grow.

I retrieved the trashcan I have stashed on the side of the desk. I bring it out and display it, as we gathered around it. She recognized the sketched figure immediately. Again, it showed in her facial expression.

As she embarked on taking a closer look, her phone beeped. She received a message and checked it. It was her mom. She was to be picking up her son for her, but was no longer able to do so at the last minute. She needed to leave so she wouldn't be late. She was apologizing as we left the room.

When she got there, she'd brought a piece of sage in, placing it on my kitchen counter. She retrieved it, stating she brought it in case any negative energy may need to be removed. She said she felt the energy was positive. There was no need to clear the home.

As I led her to the front door and exited with her, I noticed the back of her belt. Her shirt was tucked in. It was black in color, with silver metal butterflies around it. I told her how much I loved it. She stated it was from Walmart and I made a mental note. We did a quick goodbye. She would be in touch.

By now, Al has mowed our yard, the neighbors, and down by the river. He patiently awaits the return of his house as I see him heading my way. I was laughing as he was coming, because her car had precisely what he didn't want it to have on it—the advertisement.

As he pulled into the yard on the mower, he knew why I was laughing. Jokingly, with a smile, he says, "What did I tell you?" We both laughed out loud.

I didn't make it back into the house for another 30 minutes. My phone showed a missed call and voicemail when I went in. It was from Amanda. She again was apologizing for having to leave so abruptly but was bubbling with excitement about the meeting. She had such positive energy and vibes, and was looking forward to getting together again soon. She would check her schedule and be in touch.

THE SPARK I NEEDED

Between my schedule and Amanda's, we had not been able to get together. We'd been in contact via e-mails, but together time wasn't happening.

She was preparing to move, and packing was taking her time. Therefore, when the Spark of Life Fair came around, it would be the first time seeing her since our home visit.

When she was at the house, we spoke of the trashcan and how I had not added it into the book. While she saw the figure, we did not get time to discuss anything else.

Now today is the day of the fair. I am planning on seeing her there. Walking into the large conference room in the Hotel, she was sitting directly to the right of the front door. She was the second vendor lined up down the wall.

I quickly scanned the room and headed towards her table. We made small talk before I told her I would be back. She was doing card readings, and I felt I owed it to her for taking the time to come see me at home. But first, I wanted to tour the rest of the vendors.

Many tables, and people, lined the walls and center of the room—each with their own product or specialty to sell. There were natural laundry products, oils, bath salts, tea, crystal stones, jewelry, and plenty of metaphysical supplies. A reflexologist was available for massages.

All this with an effort to help people reduce stress, overcome life's obstacles, hear from a loved one, or live a happier healthier life. There were intuitive guidance readers, Oracle and Tarot card readers, clairvoyants, Psychic Mediums, and natural healing guidance vendors.

The room was full as I made my way through. It was comforting to see how many people were there. Numerous were having readings done. After completing a trip around the room, I stopped back at Amanda's table. She wanted to know if I would like a reading. I said I did.

Never having a card reading done, I wasn't sure what was next. She picked up her deck and began to shuffle them. She then wanted to know what question I had. See, I wasn't prepared. I didn't have a question lined up, or did I? I had to think a minute; a short minute, as I realized I knew the one question I needed answered.

The one driving me crazy, the one I can't let go of. The one my intuition, or gut, won't give in on. Do I add the incredible trash can with the ash figure in my book? She placed the cards on the table, closed her eyes to concentrate, and then smiled.

She stated my angels were extremely near, right over my shoulder, to be exact. I smiled, replying, "That's what I've been told." She concentrated on my question, opened her eyes and looked at me. Relaying the following message: "it comes down to you. YOU have to make the call; can you live with yourself if you don't, and can you live with the outcome if you do?" Here, I immediately knew the answer.

I could not, not tell. My inner-self, intuition, and gut have always had me captured by the fact that it was to share. It was too amazing, not too. I thanked her. We both agreed we would be in touch. I would also let her know my final decision. She wanted to read my book when it was completely finished.

I walked the room once again, purchasing the products I'd seen earlier that interested me. I bought bath salts, patchouli oil, a set of silver-plated feather earrings, and some herbal tea. I had spent my wad, but more importantly, I now felt I knew how to proceed.

I found the spark I needed, which is what I felt all along. I could not tell of the whole story. It wouldn't have been the whole truth, without it. The next day I emailed Amanda letting her know I was moving on. I would be listening to my intuition, adding it to the book.

JUNK MAIL

It was October 13th. I walked to the curb and retrieved the mail from the mailbox. I glanced at the lone envelope I retrieved, as I walked back towards the house. It was marked Personal and Confidential. It looked like junk mail.

As I finished my cigarette in the garage, I opened the envelope. It was junk mail, as I expected. But the street address of the company that sent it caught my eye on the letterhead. It had a building number of 333. The angel number, 333! Now I believe I know why I opened the letter. To see the numbers.

I entered the house and threw the envelope, and letter, on the island in the kitchen. Later in the evening, while standing there, I noticed the town's name on the outside of the envelope. It was St. Peter's, MO. St. Peter's …now my mind wanders. Is this, could this, be another sign? I grabbed my phone and headed to Google to refresh my memory of St. Peter.

ST. PETER, THE ROCK

Peter was a fisherman from Galilee. When he and Jesus first met, Jesus called him Simon Peter. The rough and reckless fisherman, in Jesus' eyes, was a firm and faithful rock. After Jesus praised him, Peter denied the Lord three times. But in the end, Peter found the courage and was willing to follow Jesus. And with this, God used him in significant ways.

Jesus taught Peter to overcome fear and put him to service. While Peter had been a failure, Jesus also knew failure was self-inflicted. Over and over, Peter needed to be taught, in patience and love. Jesus knew if Peter were willing to learn, he would be a good teacher.

As Peter, who was willing to leave all he had to follow Jesus, became the fisher of men, God used him to preach his word.

Peter, aka Simon Peter, became St. Peter, the Apostle. One of the Twelve Apostles of Jesus Christ, said to be the first Bishop, or Pope of Rome, in the Christian Church. He also became known as "The Rock."

I replaced the "sacred" trash can with the "totem of souls" from the garage, with another similar to it. Same material, same height, except this one was round. The other trash can, inside the house, was wrapped up to preserve the etchings made out of ashes.

As soon as I did it, my mind whispered why. "Why did you do that?" Why did I spit in the trash can? I had built up phlegm; there was no Kleenex in the Kleenex box. It was the closest thing I saw. Gross! It now ran down the trash can side, which brought thoughts of what appeared in the last trash can.

The next day, while in the garage, I am taken to the trash can. The area of the drippings of phlegm, down the side, has me again taking photos of the inside of yet another gross, smelly, nasty, ash-filled trash can.

I didn't wash it out the day before and now I am asking, "good God," what have you got me doing?

In awakening, I've learned there are many mystical phenomena if you are open to seeing them. This is true if you scroll inward, in a still picture one takes. Many things are hidden to the open eye but captured in the stillness of a photograph.

Now, here again, I am shown another mystical making, through ashes. While the phlegm had a look of its own, it was what I now saw off to the side of it. A face. An ancient, old, distinguished-looking face. The eyes appear to be looking upward. It carried a mustache and beard. It is then; I again head to Google. And I knew my first search.

There were many photos online as I scrolled through, not one, not two, or three, but many, many pictures. The eyes looking upward, with a hand and finger raised towards the Heavens. Here I believe I have found whom I see in my newest trashcan and photograph. St. Peter, the Prince of the Apostles. The leader of early Christians, and the one Jesus called "The Rock."

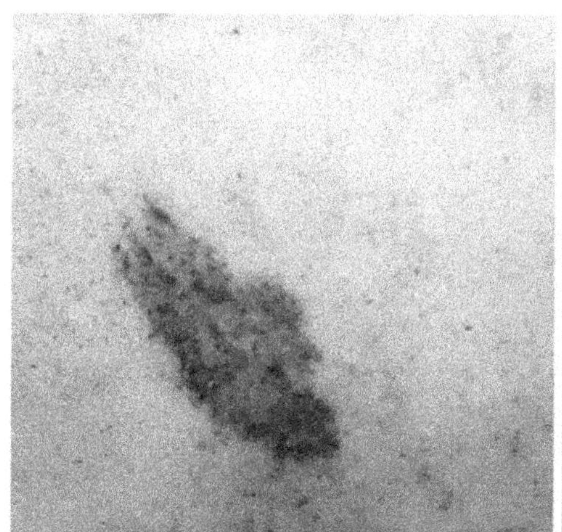

AN ANGEL KISS

Awakening takes you to God, the higher universal source, directly. You learn beyond your recognition, a reality of life not taught. But you are left feeling torn; torn between two lovers of what you were taught, what you are learning, seeing, given, in experiences, and reality.

Prayer is prayer. No matter how one prays, meditates, or worships their God. It is on their own agenda and reasoning for those prayers. Tonight I lay in bed, praying to God, my highest power, for answers.

With eyes closed, I prayed, "why, dear Lord, have you brought me here? I seek to understand. I ask for your guidance and your answers. I seek to know the truth of this journey."

It was swift. It came in and out in a flash. A ray of light, touching the left side of my forehead. It was roughly one and a half inches away when I noticed it. It came in softly, touched my forehead, and left as fast as it came.

I laid there now fully aware. My mind raced and wondered what it was. It wasn't anything, but it was something. A light, tapered inward and feathered out in length. Again, touching my forehead, with a gentle touch, and gone in a flash.

Lying there, my inner voice, told me it was that of an angel. An angel kiss. And while I didn't yet understand the true message and meaning of my journey, I felt blessed to feel the closeness, comfort, and love from God, the angels, and the other side.

He tells us when in need, He will send His angels to guard and protect us. He tells us so in Psalm 91:11. Here, I was being comforted, with the "kiss" of an angel.

"For He will order His angels to protect you wherever you go."

THE AUTOGRAPH

It was December 13th. I again found myself asking for a sign on my way home from work. A sign I'm on the right track to wherever this journey was leading me. A sign that God was truly guiding me.

I wanted something different. Something more than the triple numbers I always see. I see them so often I told myself I wanted something more powerful. Something more dominant. Something undeniable.

That night I was preparing supper. After washing potatoes to bake, I placed them on the counter. As the two potatoes laid in front of me, I am taken to some of the markings I see on one of them. In looking further, I am in awe as to what I see—my sign.

I called Al to the kitchen. Asking him "what he saw." He answered with a "G." Yes, I see a "G" as well. Staring closer, in amazement, I saw a "J" as well. At the bottom edge of the G, on the inner side end stroke, there is a J.

And I am taken to every time I wonder, or ask, I am answered. The initials placed upon my potato were my confirmation sign—a "G" for God, a J for Jesus. There is also what could appear to be a seven on the lower outside of the G.

Seven is stated to be one of the most significant numbers of the Bible. It is noted to be the number of completeness and spiritual perfection. It's said to be stamped on every work of God. It, along with HIS two initials, are on my potato. That, to me, is an autograph and is, undeniably, a powerful sign!

WHY WAS HE IGNORING ME?

We had spoken about it. He knew I wanted it. Why was he ignoring me? I looked at them at Sam's Club. I tried to show him what I would like, but he walked off. I knew there would be another book. He knew it too. I scraped by with the first book bouncing back and forth from Colton's old laptop and our desktop. Lord, why is he ignoring me?

The boys had arrived. Christmas Eve, 2016, was here. Beers and snacks were consumed, but patience is hard, probably the hardest, human thing to accept. No matter the age. Especially when gifts are involved. It was nearing 6:30 p.m., and we again found ourselves gathered in the living room, where many gifts were laid.

The boys both brought gifts, and Al placed some last-minute ones under the tree as well. I noticed his gifts were not huge boxes. Definitely not what I had been promoting for him to get me.

As is our custom, the gifts were handed out by me. Then, the youngest goes first in the opening. Oldest is last. Once the boys were done, I was next. I opened a gift from Colton first. I told him I wanted a butterfly belt like Amanda's. I told him it came from Walmart. He was successful in finding it, and I was thrilled! He also purchased the bath salts and other items I had on my list. He did so well.

Next was a gift from Chris. It was a slim, long box. My head is down, unwrapping the gift on one end. When I had the paper pulled back far enough, I could see what was written on the side of the box.

They ran. I couldn't help it. My heart was full as the tears ran down my face. I couldn't look up. I kept my head down. I was overwhelmed at the identification of the Dell Laptop that was inside. It took me a few moments before returning my focus to my family.

In looking up, they, too, are overwhelmed with feelings and happiness. The tears that fell were tears of love. Not of sadness, or guilt, or fear, but of love; it was an emotional and heartfelt moment; for all of us.

I was then told it was on Thanksgiving. We were back home with family and relatives to celebrate the Holiday. The guys were watching football, sitting around the table, checking Black Friday sales on their phones, when Al mentioned I wanted a new laptop.

This was all Chris needed to hear. Within minutes he told his dad he had one coming. And then, I knew. I knew why Al wanted no part of looking at laptops. One had already been purchased. And Chris did well. He made it happen. No wonder my husband continued to ignore me. I do love my family! I don't say it enough, but I am so incredibly blessed.

A SCULPTURED MASTERPIECE

No! We are not taking them to the dump. They are too nice. They can be refurbished. To purchase a new set like that would be $200 plus. No, you are not throwing them away!

It was a six-piece, rod-iron, patio furniture set. The last tenants at mom's condo left them for her. She had no use for them. She had her own outdoor furniture from the house that she was using.

While visiting her one weekend, I offered to get them out of her garage; Chris could use them in his backyard; he had only a few odd outdoor chairs outback. This would be perfect. A paint job and new cushions would be all it needed to bring the set to life. We took them and later delivered them to his house.

He was not as impressed with it as I was. He saw the old worn out cushions, the weathered paint, and he snubbed his nose. Each time we would visit him, the subject came up. Each time he, and his dad, would say they were going to the dump.

I was tired of hearing it. I knew if I didn't do something soon, one day I would come, and they would be gone. So, today I was taking them home. We loaded the furniture on the truck, leaving the cushions by his trash bin. They were shot.

Now I had a new project. It was February, Winter, and the cold was here, and it would be a great indoor project. When we arrived home, they were unloaded and placed in the garage. I would refurbish them there.

The next day I jumped in. Each piece was washed and cleaned of dirt and debris. I taped the sections of the back of the double chair off with paper and masking tape. It's now I am onto one of the single chairs. It is laid on its side for the ease of taping.

While taping, I come across an area on the armrest's inner side; it's a small white spot. It looks like a speck of unwanted, splattered paint. It's in the shape of a heart. I grab my phone, snap a quick photo, then continue taping.

An old sheet was placed on the floor. It had paint markings throughout it as it'd been used with previous projects. I set and adjusted the double benched chair on the sheet. It is now I see a beautiful black and white feather sticking out of the sheet. I smiled at myself because, of course, it's a sign. I do believe when feathers appear, angels or loved ones are near. I retrieved it and set it on the table.

The first coat of paint went exceptionally well and smooth. After applying and dried, I removed the masked off areas and re-taped each one to put the second color on each piece's backs. This would take protecting the areas I previously painted.

Once the second color was painted and dried, I removed all the tape and paper. I could now see if, and where, a touch up may be needed. I did see a few spots. To do the touch-up, I use a brush and a paper plate. The plate is light, flexible, and disposable. It's an easy cleanup.

I sprayed paint directly onto the plate, which gave a circle design. I started by dabbing my brush in the paint. Filling in any areas on the furniture I saw needing to be touched-up. Once done, I did a quick inspection. The pieces all looked good.

I placed the paper plate and brush on the garage table. A restroom break was needed inside. When I returned, I made one last inspection, before heading to clean my brush, and disposing of the paper plate.

Again, I was satisfied. I returned to the table to fetch the brush and to dispose of the paper plate. When I looked at the table, I am taken back by what I see. The paper plate appears to have a sculptured painting, portrayed on it.

In doing touch-up, I sprayed a round spot of paint onto the paper plate. From there, I dabbed my brush in the paint, in no particular fashion. I dabbed here, and I patted there, I stroked here and stroked there, on the paper plate, adding paint to the paintbrush.

I paid no attention to what was forming on it. But, as I now looked at it lying on the table, it appears I painted a masterpiece. A side view of a busted sculpture is displayed.

It shows what appears to be a person's head and neck. Displayed is a facial side view, showing the nose, forehead, and chin. It is shaded darker on top of the head as if hair, with a receding hairline. And in looking at it, I believe I may know who it is, I created.

On a side note, the patio furniture, with the refurbishment, had the furniture looking brand new. So new and nice, Chris did not get the furniture set back. I purchased new cushions and placed the furniture out back in my enclosed retreat area. It was perfect. I guess his continued snubs, well, was my gain.

I LOVE YOU, FOREVER

Love. The deep affection we hold for someone or something. It's a deep inner feeling and pleasure we receive from it. It is a core to life. To feel love, and give love, is fundamental to life's happiness. To hold love is both beautiful and life-changing.

With it comes acceptance, no matter the flaws; it comes with trust and deep caring. It is patient and kind. To lose someone you love is heart-wrenching. Whether through a divorce, separation, life-changes, or ones passing.

Losing a love once held brings an open wound to the heart and soul. An infliction, emotionally contained within.

May is full of family birthdays. Lenny's birthday as well. This year will be his 2nd angel-birthday in Heaven. I drove the short drive to town and the Discount Store, where I purchase cards at a discount price.

I pulled into the somewhat busy parking lot, found a spot, and parked. Exiting my vehicle, I walked down the road towards the store and entrance. It took roughly 20 minutes, and I had purchased my cards, paid, and left.

Taking the same way back to my car, I walked down the parking lot road. Nearing my vehicle, I see a piece of clothing, or something, lying in the middle of the street. It is directly in my walking path. I passed it up, then quickly stopped. My mind replayed and registered what I saw.

Turning around, I walked back to take a better look at the material item lying in the street. It's white, with black lettering. There are red hearts throughout. The wording said what I thought it said. I picked the item up.

The material displays, "I love you forever" in writing. There are hearts displayed for the o's in the word love. I looked around the parking lot, searching for anyone who may have dropped it. There is no one in sight.

I returned to my vehicle with the item. Sitting inside, I admired the piece of fabric. I now see it's a blanket for an infant car seat carrier. The I love you written throughout, and the hearts were a beautiful sign someone was sending me love. And my guess would be Lenny, whom I didn't get to buy a birthday card for today.

It was heartwarming. It wasn't lying there when I went into the store. Upon my return, it is mystically lying directly in my path. I couldn't miss it. My eyes wanted to swell with tears. I loved the love and communication from spirit. It has proven to be so healing and comforting in my grief.

I sat silently, telling them, "I loved them too." I was appreciative of the abundance of signs of their eternal love. It was a real, healing blessing. But damn, I missed them here.

ANGELIC PLACEMENT

The solid wood desk in the office was big and tall. The desk was a Christmas gift for Chris when he was a teenager. It's a big man's desk, he used for multiple screens, with his gaming. It's so big; he didn't take it with him when he moved out. He didn't have room.

Nor did he take it when he moved into his new home. He again said he didn't have room, nor did he need it. We kept it in our office and continued to use it. I'd raise the computer chair up as far as it would go but always found myself straining, looking up, at the screen.

It wouldn't take long, and the kink in the back of my neck would appear. With another book in writing, I was looking for a better, more comfortable, working place. The laptop could go anywhere. Today, I played around in the living room, with the furniture.

I took our coffee table, placing it long-ways, up against the far end of the couch. I put a small end table up against the coffee table. A small leather footstool was placed in front of it for sitting. It sat low to the ground, but I hoped it would be better than the large, uncomfortable office desk.

Once all was in place, I added my laptop to the small end table. I found myself sitting on the stool at the newly make-shift desk. I'd placed my notebook, paperwork, and a bill on the coffee table.

My first agenda was to call on the increased bill. I make the call with my cell phone and have been put on hold. As I waited for a human voice to come on the phone, my elbow, or "entity," inadvertently hit my driver's license, which was lying loosely on the coffee table as well—knocking it off the table.

I have the phone in my left hand, and to my ear, looking for it directly below me. I didn't see it there. I didn't see it bending over on the stool, looking under the coffee table and the small end table. Now I stood to search harder. I was inspecting the entire vicinity.

Then, I see it. It's not lying on the floor, as I assumed it would be. My first written memorial book, "Signs for my Soul," sits on the coffee table slates on the bottom; next to it is our Holy Bible. My Driver's License is laying on top of my book.

It's laying in unison with the cross that sits upon it. The cross is centered on the book cover, and my driver's license, with my name, birth date, and photo, is faced upward, in the lower part of the cross. This would be the farthest area from where it was knocked off.

I became suspicious if it was my elbow that knocked the Driver's License off the table or was it something else. I wasn't sure how it happened. I just saw it go flying.

Finding its placement, aligned precisely, evenly, with the cross, can only be described as being prestigiously placed, in an angelic way. The identification I use in life, my name, my DOB, strategically placed, on my book, as if for a reason. I took photos upon finishing my telephone call.

THE ANGEL FLIGHT

Why did we miss our scheduled flight? We ran like hell to catch the plane. After the delays, it would be close. When we arrived, the plane was there, but the door had been closed. Unable to be opened. We stood there together, four of us left behind, watching the airplane back out of the terminal. Leaving us stranded, with no current way home.

We'd been to San Francisco for an annual conference; it was our return trip home. We landed in Dallas, and an hour later, we found ourselves miles away from the airport, checking into a tiny, small, aged, motel.

Due to the flight delays in San Francisco and the wait to land and taxi, it would be close. Many on the flight had already missed their connecting flights. Others, like us, would have to hurry like hell to meet theirs.

It was terminals away. We ran the escalator stairs. Jumped on the tram and hoped. Hoped we would be on time. It was 9:00 p.m., and we anxiously wanted to be home in our bed. We ran the long corridors, gate by gate, with hope.

But, as we, and two other guys, running to catch the plane with us, saw the plane and heard the news, we were left with a realization that we were not getting on the plane and going home tonight. The door had been closed and could not be reopened. I wanted to cry!

The Hotel they placed us in was miles away. We were given vouchers for taxi rides. It was the 5th taxi we approached, who finally agreed to take us with the coupons. In accepting them, the company must send it to the airline for payment. It was obvious; no one wanted to wait for 2-weeks to receive their money.

We received food vouchers as well, for dinner. They, too, were not taken by the few restaurant choices we had to eat. It was 10:30 p.m. So after the hassle of finding a taxi to take them and the first fast food place, we resigned to the fact they were useless.

On our walk to find food, I mentioned everything happens for a reason. Sometimes we just don't know what the reason is. As we stood at the crosswalk, waiting to cross the highway, a vehicle pulled up at the stoplight: the tag number is 222.

Our suitcase whereabouts were unknown. We had no toiletries or clothes. Only what we were wearing. It was a short night's sleep. We were up at dawn, headed back down the Interstate Highway, to get to the airport and our flight home.

The plane was full on the early morning flight to Manhattan. The two stewards introduced themselves and the safety procedures, as the plane taxied the runway. The stewards were a lady and a man. I paid no attention to her, but I did him when he introduced himself.

We didn't get to sit together. Al, and I. He sat in the seat in front of me. One of the other stranded guys from last night sat with him. I laughed out loud when the steward announced his name. I could see and hear; Al had chuckled as well.

The flight was smooth and a short hour away. As we drew closer to home and landing, he came on to thank us. He thanked us for flying with him, and The Angel Flight. His name, in which he announced earlier, was Angel.

And so, in what was our unfortunate misfortune, I could only believe, we were once again, exactly where we were meant to be. Everything happens for a reason. This reason was for us to be flying, on The Angel Flight, home.

DISCOVERY

Part II

THE VOYAGE

When the caterpillar thought its life was over, it found its wings, opened them, and became a butterfly!

As I was ready to put the cruise control on life, I found myself swimming for an unknown shore. The boys were no longer home. We no longer had the daily responsibilities of parenting, and retirement was inching closer and closer.

It was here, life bestowed before me, treacherous waves, in the deep, vast ocean. It sent me overboard, from my gentle ride, into the cold, dark waters; it took all my energy and effort to stay afloat and swim for safety and life.

There was only one I knew to summon. He was the only one who could, in my reality, keep me afloat, from going under. He was the one I learned to call to keep me from sinking myself into the tides of despair and darkness.

Once I put out the S.O.S, He arrived quickly, bringing His survival promise and energy. The air He produced inflated my deflated life vessel. He took hold, guiding me to safety. My worries about my brother's destination faded fast. A calmness took over my inner being.

I began to see and swim towards a new light. Believing my brother was safe on the other side. The messages, and signs received, confirmed a higher presence was with me, safely guiding me.

I'd driven the short two blocks from work to the small City Park. It was a frequent place I came to eat on my mini-30-minute lunch hour. It was a straight drive, turning right, from the office driveway exit.

As I approached the park, on the third block, I drove forward through the intersection. Slowly inching over to the curb, coming to a stop, I put my car in park and turned the keys off.

That day, I didn't bring lunch with me. I had leftovers, but I left them at the office. I would eat them later. Today, I sat in my vehicle, closed my eyes, and I prayed. I prayed to God for my brother's son Andrew, his family, and friends. They were preparing to say goodbye to Lenny in Las Vegas today.

I prayed for Lenny and his body's safe travels to Kansas. I prayed for Andrew's safe flight. And I prayed and cried for the loss of my brother. The death of a loved one is the hardest thing we will survive in life. Losing a loved one takes an inner piece of our heart with them.

It's not something you get over; as they say, you learn to get through it. Suicide made it even harder in the thought of the afterlife. There, in the unknown, I found myself asking, praying to God for a sign. I received "Flowers from Heaven" later that day.

I left work at 5:00 p.m. and stopped by the store to get a few items for supper. After paying I turned to put my wallet back into my purse as a young gal approached me, her arms extended towards me, holding flowers. Three tulips, two red and one pink.

She asked if I wanted them. I was in awe. I gestured to take them from her, letting her know I most definitely wanted them. I thanked her and placed them on top of my purse, as if they were holy. For me, they were my answer, my sign, from above.

With that, my spiritual awakening, and transformational voyage began. The definition of transformation, according to Dictionary.com. is "the act or process of transforming, the state of being transformed. Change in form, appearance, nature, or character." While transformation can be of anything, it is in life; we are given the power to transform our minds, choices, and reality.

That day, in faith, my transformation took center stage. The mere thought of receiving flowers to my request was pure bliss. God had sent them through someone. I had no choice but to believe.

In this voyage, I was enlightened too; if we forgive and let go of things we cannot change or control, we open space to make mental and energetic life changes. Letting go opens space in our mind and body, allowing for new energy, positivity in life, and health.

The mind is spoken of to be like an open camera. Capturing everything it sees, feels, senses, and experiences. This camera does not have a shut-off button. Nor does it have a delete button. It runs, and runs, holding everything on backup. It is up to us to pause that button. Otherwise, events throughout life continue to run in the background, open, in the subconscious, triggering an emotion repeatedly in similar incidences.

Anxiety and depression can be diagnosed from living in the past and into the future. Thoughts of past occurrences or future ones disconnect one from the heart and soul. This due to the constant thought process in the repetition of past situations and traumas or future outcomes.

In other words, we worry too much about what happened yesterday, last year, and what may happen tomorrow. That's life, right? I know that was me, for sure. I was never in this/the now and present moment. To enjoy what was happening in the current time

I was strengthened by my faith, thankful for what I had, in life, and in all moments. I knew I was well, I was enough, and I was loved. It became my own lifeboat, on the voyage.

THE CHANGE ~ THE SHIFT

If you do nothing, nothing will change!

That statement. "If you do nothing, nothing will change." It echoed in my mind, through my heart, and to my soul. Change. What needed to change? Besides quitting smoking, I don't know what else I could or would need to change.

Life was content; I was abundantly blessed, having a caring, loving, and supporting husband. Our boys were growing into fine young gentlemen; I had my family. I lived in a lovely home and was abundantly blessed. I'd had great rewarding professional jobs, with opportunities to travel to extraordinary cities and events. I wasn't understanding.

While one talks of the change, it may dominantly be spoken with the evolution of life. The time when a woman experiences menopause and the end of fertility. The end of the reproductive period, and menstruating.

My night sweats were extreme. I was waking nightly to full-body sweats. The sheets hot, damp and moist, from perspiration. The pillow sheets stuck to the back of my neck. It was interrupting and playing havoc with my sleep.

I previously attributed them to the womanly hormonal menopause. But now, I think the episodes could be related to anxiety in my dreams. The ones I was once told I was having, but not remembering.

It is now I've noticed the hot sweat breakouts during the day as well. I initially related them to "hot flashes." Now, as I speak of new spiritual experiences to Al, the hot perspiration rushes swept over me. I was becoming aware of what was triggering my senses into the hot flashes.

The moist, wet perspiration would overcome my head and face. An instant, sweat swept over my body. Now, I was correlating them to a stressful situation, event, and anxiety. Not due to the womanly change in life. Not due to my feminine character. But due to stress that arose in my senses.

We know in truth, not one of us wants to be told we need to change. It's a hit on our ego. While there are things we all would rather have differently or would like to quit, or change, about ourselves, or our situations, we don't want to hear it from anyone. In my case, I hadn't a clue, what the Spiritual Advisor meant, in change, or why.

When told, it stuck to me like a piece of gum on the bottom of my shoe. I couldn't unstick it. I needed to know more. Being introduced to the chakras, I immediately became engulfed in online studies.

Merriam-Webster Dictionary defines a chakra as "any of several physical or spiritual energy points in the human body according to yoga philosophy. The human body has more than 88,000 points of physical or spiritual energy."

In Hinduism, there are seven main chakras. Each is associated with a color, shape, sense, organ, natural element, deity, and mantra. These may align us with the life force spirit energy. I also found a multitude of other energy healing techniques in my discovery.

In Chinese culture, it is chi, or qi, in which life force is stated to derive from; the Yin and Yang. The meridian system in which life energy flows. Prana is another Hindu philosophy, including yoga, Indian medicine, and Indian martial arts; the Sanskrit word for "life force" or vital principle constructed from pra, meaning movement, and constant.

Acupuncture is an energy technique. It stimulates the energy by inserting needles through the skin at over 88,000 specific points. Reflexology focuses on balancing the qi but primarily targets the hands, ears, and feet. EFT is a popular tapping therapy, which is called Emotional Freedom Tapping.

In Buddhism, mindfulness, meditation, concentration, and insight are said to carry energy healing. Many think and believe Buddhism is a religion, when, in fact, it is not. It is a practice—a mindfulness practice.

Reiki is another known energy technique. It's the use of one's hands and palms to transfer, balance, and realign energy from the healer to the recipient. It comes from the recurrent concept of unseen life force that flows between us, channeled and used for beneficial means.

This technique, developed by Japanese Mikao Usui, was based on five principles. Don't get angry; don't worry, be grateful, work diligently, and be kind to others. In Japanese, the known energy force is ki.

A search for energy healing in the Bible came up empty. Yet we do know Jesus was a healer. He performed miracles by touching and praying with His hands, transforming many diseases and lives. He healed and preached His word, through the "I am."

In the practice of chakra energy healing, I AM affirmations, are daily rituals of self-empowerment, an oath to an action or process affirming something. There are different affirmations for each chakra.

These affirmations, when repeated, can change your mind, consciousness, and energy in you. The I AM's are said to be the two most essential words in life, for what you place behind them becomes your reality.

In energy healing, positive self-affirmations are critical in which one may revive and recharge their life force energy and mental reality. Affirmations are self-empowerment statements in which one tells oneself; to give themselves self-love, self-confidence, self-compassion, and self-worth; mantra's work the same way.

Here is where you can begin to love yourself; to revive your energy source. Without telling ourselves complimentary messages, we may never, ever, receive any positive interaction. When we speak to ourselves with positivity, it impacts our energy—having a significant effect on our life, health, and love.

My change began with my newest place, outdoors. Energy healing was in the sun, in nature, reaping the free Vitamin D. It was in quietness, forgiveness, and affirmations. This was the changer; these were the battery chargers and healers.

It was easy to become addicted to nature. The birds were happily chirping, the squirrels sassily squawking their tune. The sound of the gentle wind through the leaves, feeling the softness of the light breeze. The warmth of the shining sun in the sky belting down.

The magical clouds that hovered overhead. After a storm, the calmness, or the smell of the rain, captured me in my senses. The flowers were blooming, their fragrance in the air. The animals, the critters, their characters, their nature. All so healing, and all so free.

It happened quickly, the shift. From then forward, I began to feel the stillness in the outdoors, minus human noise in the environment. I realized why we built the screened enclosed porch outback. It was meant to be.

It would be my reprieve, and my oasis, in healing. Evenings were spent on the swing by the fire pit in the yard or inside the enclosed porch. It's screened in 3/4 the way up, with wooden plywood covering the lower half. It is stained and decorated in rustic attire; it's an amazing retreat to nature.

The Cicada is a well-known insect in Kansas in the summer months, that may also be called locusts. Their loud voices echo through the air with their harmonious buzz around sunset. And then, in an instant, like a switch being turned off, they stop. It is simultaneously coordinated, it appears.

This is how I would make the shift, bringing me inner peace and wellness. It is in the outdoors, in God's beautiful tapestry, where healing and energy thrive. He has provided us with the healing and spiritual elements all around us, if one is open to seeing it, and utilizing it.

NEAR-DEATH EXPERIENCE (NDE)

The ranch house was a square boxed, one level, two-bedroom home; the kitchen was a sizable double-sized room, with an open floor plan. The living room, and bedrooms, all entered into it. The bathroom was another doorway, which went to the laundry room, and a long, narrow, enclosed entry porch.

We'd been taken there in Al's oil field job. We were moving from the Panhandle of Oklahoma to Miami, TX. Our friends had moved there earlier. Al and he both worked for the same oil company. Their boss recommended the house for us when we decided to make a move.

He knew a couple who were looking for tenants. The house was in the country, on a Ranch. The couple lived there and were the ranch hands. We took the drive, roughly 15 miles outside of town, to see if it was for us.

The main house was visible from the entrance of the drive. Large cattle lots, filled with cattle, covered the grounds after that. Further down the road, off the dirt trail, sat the other house for rent. It was white and well kept on the outside. The yard was large, green, and well maintained.

Inside, the floors were a white tile; there was no carpet throughout. The rooms painted white as well. The large open living room carried numerous long, single-paned windows along the walls-it was older, but well-kept. We took it.

That particular evening in 1983, we were watching TV in the living room. I was comfortably lying on the couch. Al was in his recliner. In an instant, I felt the feeling of needing to use the restroom. I rose and entered the kitchen that led towards the bathroom.

Once there, I sat to use the stool. A sudden pain appeared in my left side, along with feeling dizzy. It had me making a loud call for Al. Next thing I recall; I am laying on the cold tile floor. Al is on his knees at my side.

While unconscious, I saw the vision of my dad extending his hand to me. As if welcoming me across to the other side. In my discoveries and research, I've found this could be considered a near-death experience.

A near-death experience is portrayed to be an unusual experience taking place on the brink of death, recounted by a person after recovery. One may experience a meeting of a dead family member or friend.

Once I came to, he picked me up, attempting to carry me through the kitchen, towards the bedroom. Two steps into the kitchen, I relayed the need to use the restroom. Quickly! An abrupt turn-around took us back towards the bathroom. But not in time.

My bowels released before getting there, making it very unpleasant. It was a mess, a bloody mess, at that—front abdominal cramping set in. After a call by Al to the small hospital ER, 30-minutes away, it was decided it may be worth waiting until morning. There was no on-call doctor. One would be there in the morning.

The night was long. Anxiety and fear stormed through me; the continued attempts to make it to the restroom continually failed-each with the bloody, red, watery liquid. The cramping kept me huddled, in a fetal position, throughout the night. There was no sleep, only fear, pain, blood, and tossing.

It was around 6:00 a.m., and we are in the vehicle, driving the 30-minute drive to the closest hospital. Upon arrival, I darted for the restroom. Al visits with the nurse and obtains paperwork. I am in no condition to complete it as he attempts to answer the questions. Back and forth to the restroom I would go.

The wait was distant until I was called back to an exam room. My underwear was ruined, wet, and disgusting; my jeans as well. A pad was given to me earlier, which was soiled. I laid on the hospital bed, awaiting something to relieve my pain and the horrible symptoms.

A doctor came in around 8:30 a.m. Urine was taken, blood drawn, and IV's administered. A colonoscopy, an inner view of the intestines, was needed and scheduled for late morning. Medications were ordered and distributed to slow down the stools and the intense lower abdominal cramping pain.

There was a colonoscopy prep, which was given to clean me out. I inquired how I could have anything else left in me. It was protocol, I was told. The pre-op liquid antidote, nasty in taste, came up as fast as it went down. The procedure, performed later that morning, was a trauma in itself.

There was no option to be sedated for the medical procedure, so I wasn't. With all that had gone on throughout the night and the procedure, I was left physically, mentally, and emotionally depleted.

Labs were continually taken and being monitored. Earlier results confirmed I was one-point away from a blood transfusion. The long night of blood loss endured was apparent. Thankfully, the meds being administered now, were taking control. They were stopping the episodes, avoiding the need for blood.

A diagnosis of the colonoscopy would be Irritable Bowel Syndrome, colitis, and spastic colon. The next two days I spent in the hospital, regaining fluids, and strength. Our friends came to visit me the next day. It was weeks later when she stated she was "shocked" when she saw me that day. She said, "I was white as a ghost." The blood loss was evident.

IBS (Irritable Bowel Syndrome) is described as a large intestine problem, causing abdominal cramping, bloating, gas, diarrhea, or constipation. The next year was spent with a monthly visit to the doctor's office.

Anti-spasm meds were continued daily, four times a day. After that, I was dismissed, and the meds were prescribed and used on an as-needed basis. When cramping and bloating would occur, which was more than not. The need for the medication became a daily part of life.

I would be hospitalized two more times with IBS, once in the 1990s and again in 2005. The symptoms, the same. Cramping and bloody stools without control. Diagnosis' were focal colitis and ischemic colitis, which means bloody stools.

There were colonoscopies every three years, in between. In the prep work, it would shock my system in the cleaning out process. I would fashionably pass out. This occurred every time. The anxiety I carried gave it an extra boost. I would worry about the prepping procedure and the possibility of passing out again. And I would.

THE BLACK TONGUE

In 1978, I began working in the dental office. I was asked to apply for the job and got it. It was such a blessing. As a dental assistant, one becomes accustomed to cleaning and checking their teeth, gums, and mouth. It's what we do.

On this particular early morning, in 1979, I found myself in front of the mirror. I was opening my mouth wide to look in. Here I saw my tongue, in the reflection. The top layer's sight was covered in a dark, black color. It took my heart to my stomach. Why the…what the…was going on? Why in the world was my pink tongue black?

I hurried, seeking out my boss, the dentist. He was in the lab, in between patients. He took a look, examining my tongue. He questioned if I'd taken any antacids the night before? My response, "I took some Pepto. Did that count?"

I awoke in the middle of the night, with a pain in my upper gut. It was extreme enough to get up and take a chug on the stomach ache pain medicine bottle; this would be my first recollection of the upper stomach gut pain; heartburn?

As years went by, it persisted, increasingly waking me in the night. So much so, in the late 1990s, I sought treatment. After testing, the diagnosis was the gallbladder. Diagnostic tests completed reported the gallbladder showed only a 29% ejection fraction.

In 2001, I had surgery, and my gallbladder was removed. In recovery from the cholecystectomy procedure, I awoke in horrible pain. It was in the same upper gut area that had brought me to have surgery. It was extreme and intensified.

The recovery nurses assessed me, administering pain medications in the IV on my hand. I dozed off. Awakened shortly after that, I was transferred to the outpatient area and settled into a recliner for recovery.

I was left to rest, with crackers and a soda to drink. Anesthesia hadn't been a problem in my kidney surgery, but now I found myself vomiting in the trash can next to the chair. The crackers and drink had not settled well.

I was discharged to go home a couple of hours later, though the vomiting persisted. The drive home had my head and stomach spinning. Arriving in the driveway, I abruptly opened the car door to relieve myself again; I spent the rest of the day in bed. A large kettle was next to it.

I was so prepared to be ridden of the upper gut pain. Yet, the removal of the gallbladder set off an ultimate life force battle. The pain excelled, causing additional testing with other doctors and specialist's appointments—all with no relief, definitive answers, or cure.

After several months and check-up appointments, with ongoing pain and complaints, the surgeon attributed my pain and problem to my smoking. I was in shock. In his opinion, it was the cause of my pain. A non-smoking speech was given, along with the health statistics of smoking. Which is, of course, it's terrible for you.

I was prescribed a prescription for an antidepressant that helps reduce the urge to smoke. I was, in truth, flabbergasted when I left. I was a legal assistant at the time. His impression, I thought, came across like I was going to sue him. Like I thought he did something wrong. I could sense it in how he was responding to me. Now, I will call it the vibes. The feeling you get from an incident or persons energy.

I agreed to try the anti-smoking drug. I'd tried to quit many times. It was a challenge. Six months would be the most extended timeframe. After ten days of taking the drug, I stopped. My nights were restless; the medication was keeping me awake; I couldn't sleep.

Next, I saw a gastroenterologist, undergoing an endoscopy, chest x-rays, and more appointments. The esophagus was normal in appearance, along with the stomach. The diagnosis was suspected to be related to esophageal spasms.

A spasm is described as a sudden involuntary muscular contraction or movement—a sudden violent muscular contraction of pain. A Charlie horse is a spasm. When the muscle, generally in the leg, or foot, cramps up. Here one can massage, stretch the leg, or foot, to help restrict the pain.

There is no physical way to massage, bend, or alleviate the gut squeezing, twisting, knife stabbing spasms of the muscle in esophageal spasms. The episodes were now controlling my every move. The surgery caused the epigastric pain I initially had to be unbearable.

The sharp, intense pain radiated through from the front gut area, into my back. In the beginning, it was more dominant in the early a.m. hours, waking me. But now it could come at any time of the day and night.

I sought another specialist, out of town, for a second, or was it a third or fourth opinion? I'd seen plenty. He gave me 10 minutes of his time. He walked in, stating he looked over and reviewed my medical records. Everything looked normal. There was nothing he could do for me. The surgeon who did my surgery did everything right; he then walked out of the exam room.

I was stunned and undeniably defeated. I didn't even get to speak besides saying hello. I wasn't there to know if the surgeon who did my gallbladder surgery did it right. I assumed he did. I was there to find answers, to taking away the excruciating pain I was living with.

Drinking or eating helped take away the knife stabbing, contraction; and then again, sometimes, it took a while. Prescription probiotics (gut health), channel blockers (BP/Cardio), nitro-statins (chest pain), and another antidepressant, all prescribed. All to no prevail.

One day, when picking up another new medication, I asked the pharmacist if there was a liquid I could drink that would numb my esophagus in these moments, to take away the sudden intense pain. She wasn't aware of one.

Numerous times it occurred in the vehicle. With no liquids or food to ingest. Once on a ride home from seeing family in Wichita. Its magnitude and intensity had me in yet another miserable incident.

The upper gut pain was overbearing. We had no food or drinks in the vehicle. A feeling of sickness overcame me. A restroom stop was needed. In my experience with my

IBS, I knew I couldn't wait long. My hands grasped at the seat, my body slumping over, searching for comfort. I was an overwhelming, sad mess.

Words were exchanged en route. I desperately needed to stop; he had nowhere to turn off. The first exit available, which seemed eternal, he veered down the off exit ramp. It was a lone, small, dingy, convenience store; off a non-busy exit.

I exited out of the vehicle before it came to a complete stop, sprinting to the restroom. Luck was with me. The restroom door on the old building side did not require going inside the building to get the key.

When I returned to the car, I didn't speak of what I left behind. It was uncontrollable. The remaining ride home was quiet; using the bathroom alleviated the painful upper gut spasm and sickness feeling.

Another awful incident was a casino girl's night out with my mom and sister. We'd been playing the slots and having drinks. It was late evening, around 9:00 p.m. when I felt the upper gut pain coming on. I stated I wasn't feeling well and was headed to the room.

The pain, again, miserably gut-wrenching. It squeezed, and knotted, in my upper gut. I found myself on the stool, sweat pouring from me. I stripped down, removing all my clothes. I was light-headed and went for the floor in hopes of not passing out and falling.

I wanted my sister to come to the room, but I didn't. I wanted help, but I didn't want to be seen like this. Besides, what could be done? I laid on the cold tile floor, stark naked—drinking water in attempts to stop and relieve the intense pain.

Without relief, I dressed, forcing myself in a dazed walk down the long hall to the soda machines, hoping the carbonation of a 7-Up would help. With it, the intensity began to subside after nearly a two-hour episode.

I laid quietly in my bed when my sister came to the room. I wasn't asleep, nor did I speak. At this time, I was not taking any meds for the upper gut pain. After numerous medication attempts, nothing was successful.

In the morning, I told them I got sick but did not go into the details. A few hours later on our two-hour trip home, I found myself in another episode. We were driving on I-70, headed West, towards Salina, and home. The pain began an hour in, which was a few miles before the first Manhattan exit. I was in the backseat of mom's Crossover vehicle.

The pain was back. Again, in full force. I felt sick, with the need to vomit, but only dry heaved into an empty water bottle, which I found on the vehicle floor. I climbed into the very rear of the vehicle, lying down in the small, compact area. Huddled up, trying to help alleviate the pain.

Junction City was the first reasonable exit to pull off to purchase a drink or food. The Manhattan exits would take a 20-minute drive to get to town. Junction City would be about the same timeframe, and we wouldn't have to backtrack.

We questioned back and forth a couple of times on if she should pull off. I didn't know. I just hurt. They didn't know, and before I/we knew it, we'd driven past the exits. The opportunity to pull off, for food or drink, was missed.

I continued laying in the back rear of the vehicle, praying for relief, until we arrived a few blocks from home. I then climbed back up into the back seat. As we pulled into the driveway, I rushed to exit the vehicle, opening the door. Slouched over in pain, we did a quick goodbye exchange.

The kitchen and the refrigerator were my stop upon entering the house. Grabbing the jug of milk, I gulped it down, from the container. I grabbed and ate a couple of cookies, then took myself to bed. The pain subsided, and I fell asleep, mentally and physically, exhausted, again.

The incidents were all too often. Now, in going back in time, this pain took me back to 1979, and the black tongue. Gallbladder surgery would exacerbate the problem. I've now discovered the pain was in the solar plexus's area—the third chakra.

HUMAN CHAINS

In awakening, I feel life can be summoned up as a human body, with chains. From the time we are born, through the years, chains are continually applied to us. The childhood age of growing up years, continuing into adulthood, constant routines of school, work, paying bills, money, kids, love, hate, health, worry, judgment, ego, anxiety, and death; all are attaching to us like mud on a tire, on a wet and muddy dirt road. Yes, these human chains.

The added extra weight, slowing us down, moment by moment, day by day. The traumatic memories along the way, building up in our threads, playing with the distance of our journey through life. They slow down our mind, inner peace, health, and livelihood. Driving us to the depths of illness, self-destructive hell-on-earth, and into death.

These attached chains, from childhood, family traits, ancestors, society, teachers, friends, and our inner voice; chains from challenges bestowed upon our self, aka self-inflicted. As if willingly taking a wrong turn, knowing it is the wrong destination, but going anyway.

Some chains are passed onto us from our ancestors and genetics. Through the Tree of Life and DNA, we are granted traits and diseases. Through childhood, growing up, friendships, enemies, acquaintances, and jobs, chains of judgment and acceptability are continually being attached.

Removing them means one thing, freedom, freedom to drive out of the rut and into a new landscape. Forgetting where you've been, moving steadily forward, riding the road, believing the destination you desire is up ahead. Leaving behind, shedding off the treads of life programming, history, ancestral, and socialization chains.

These heavy human chains weighed on my shoulders and life, keeping me from living good health and well-being. Those chains attached in anxiety, and fear, in sharing the whole story, at first. It was easy for my mind to tell me what appeared, and what I was experiencing wasn't a familiar road. It wasn't a route society was in-tuned to.

But, I learned to navigate my way through the unknown roads ahead. I had to let go of where I'd been and accept where I was in my path, with the driving force of my inner-self, intuition, and faith.

With it came the shedding of many threads, myths, theories, and life events, which I passed on the way. And by doing so, I came to understand that if I didn't share the actual happenings, I would continue to live with chains of fear; fear of not believing in my inner-self, heart, and soul.

Fear of what my mind had attached to it in judgment over the roads of life and life's path ahead. But most importantly, it would mean I didn't have faith in myself or my Creator. I wouldn't be honoring my true self.

So I continued in removing my chains, healing my inner-self. I moved forward, in the guidance, in faith, for me. With it came a belief of a purpose; a calling. The gentleman in *Captured by the Holy Spirit*, reading the book with the title caption, "You have been Called," was an exhibit.

Evidence had me following on the path, in light of seeing my lighted road ahead. I always accepted what I was receiving and the road I was led to. It was God's grace. The coincidences, the angel numbers, and mystical timings and places were all messages from God, the Universe, Angels, and spirit. And I came to yearn for where they were taking me.

Now, as I sat in the small office today, reading the quote, "Become famous for finishing important, difficult tasks," I knew the quote was accurate. The task of the next book appeared to be yet another difficult task. But I also knew I had the power, the energy, and guidance, leading me towards a new scenery, a new road, where chains are no longer required—and I'm not about to stop now.

THE NEED IS GONE

I often wondered why I couldn't have written a juicy love story. Something everyone would fall in love with. Over time, I began to understand, my story was a love story—my love story, of learning to love myself.

Of course, that was silly. I loved myself. We all love ourselves, right? Yet, here I am, confessing, in truth. Once upon a time, or two, my husband would jokingly state, "I don't think you even love me no more." On those few occurrences, I would simply say, "I don't love myself today; how can I love you?"

Because some days are straightforward difficult and, so maybe now, I realize the truth of my response to that statement. What one goes through daily in our lives is put at the forefront of our lives and mind. It affects our inner-self, inner-love, inner-happiness, and energy.

After a day at work, dealing with society, people, co-workers, and multiple personalities, and vibes (energy), some days, it's downright hard. Trying to satisfy people all day takes away from any loving energy left at the end of the day, for yourself or others. It's easy to come home at 5:00 p.m., with a feeling of no love to give.

It's in the emotions and experiences we endure daily that stay within; in good and bad, we hold that presence in our memory. The good brings unforgettable memories, feelings, and joy. The bad affects our everyday personalities, reactions, movements, ego's, emotions, and energy.

All come from our experiences and senses. Happy times and memories bring joy in the love you hold for the person or event. The same goes for the bad times. They too, are your senses at work.

The emotions that come with unfavorable and detrimental events left in our minds. It leaves a voice echoing judgment, perception, and self-doubt within. This voice repeats every move, action, day, week, or time, bringing the mental mind to unhappy emotions, anxiety, and depression. These thoughts take away our joy, our health, and our self-esteem.

To me, it's the devil side of the brain that speaks through negativity, doubt, ego, and hate. The Christ side of the brain communicates through kindness, caring, giving, joy, and love. On one side, we have the good; on the other, we have the bad. An old Cherokee saying is:

"One evening, an elderly Cherokee brave told his grandson about a battle that goes on inside people.

He said, "My son, there is a battle of two wolves inside us all. One is evil. It is anger, jealousy, greed, resentment, and ego.

"The other is good. It is joy, peace, love, hope, humility, kindness, empathy, and truth."

The grandson thought about it for a minute and then asked his grandfather: "Which wolf wins?"

The old Cherokee simply replied, "The one you feed."

Cherokee Proverb

Our brain, which travels with us all places, brings emotions from our senses. Weighing in the battle that goes on inside. Negative experiences can produce the "fight and flight response." Our reactions to life events, stress, fear, and challenging life emotions play one side of the two wolves. It is here the "fight and flight response" kicks in.

Fight and flight response is defined in the Merriam Webster dictionary as "relating to being or causing physiological changes in the body, (such as an increase in heart rate or dilation of bronchi) in response to stress.

It is a reaction that occurs in response to a perceived harmful event, attack, or threat to survival. It is associated with the amygdala. The amygdala is a center in the brain responsible for emotions and emotional behaviors."

In recognizing my sweat breakouts while talking of new spirit experiences to Al, I came to understand; I was in a "fight or flight" situation, causing the hot, perspiration, flashes. I was anxious, in the telling, causing the threat of judgment to my experience.

The brain holds everything, good and bad, habits, experiences, and memories, storing them in our subconscious mind. While this is how we understand life to be, it is now I know it doesn't have to be that way.

The removal of old emotions and attachments, which is known as "brain fog" or "monkey mind," diminishes the lower emotional energy of old experiences. This makes room for new positive energy. Positive energy is healing energy. In awakening, your efforts work to quiet the monkey brain and brain fog.

Consciousness is defined in Merriam-Webster as "the quality or state of being aware especially of something within oneself; the state or fact of being conscious of an external object, state, or fact. Awareness, especially: concern for some social or political cause."

While the subconscious never shuts down, it is in the conscious mind to rest it, and the full-time thoughts. When it runs full steam and holds steady feelings, resentment, anxiety, fear, and the need for approval, it can manifest into the diseases we may acquire on life's path.

The subconscious mind manifests worries, fear, guilt, lies, and grief into illness. And so may the conscious mind manifest good things into wellness. To quiet the brain is to quiet the never-ending thoughts—something I never knew you could do.

In the late '90s, I sought the help of anxiety medication from my doctor. Life; my health, motherhood, wifehood, working; all were weighing on me, my emotions, and anxiety and fears. I sought something to calm me down, something to help me sleep.

In bed, my mind wondered. It went through the day's events, tomorrow's expectations, and constant worries. My subconscious roamed wild, deep in the day's events, feelings, and what if's—concerns of life.

But I was learning self-love and the power of the mind. I began to speak, talk, and silence that inner voice, rambling full-time inside my head. Bedtime was now my time. It was no longer a time to sweat what did happen, or what most likely would not happen tomorrow or in the future.

I could no longer let my mind run havoc over me. Bedtime was not the time to lay and worry. It was my time and sleep time. After nightly prayer, I listened to meditations lying in bed.

The quietness of headphones, the softness of the voice or tone, took the mind away from thought. All were quieting my mind away from the infectious mental chatter; it was a time of making the mind step-away, into peaceful, relaxing, calmness, and peace, into sleep. There was not a thing I could do at that moment, that would change a darn thing. Luke 12:22-26 tells us:

"Do not worry about your life, what you will eat; or about your body, what you will wear. Life is more than food and the body more than clothes. Consider the ravens: they do not sow or reap, they have no storeroom or barn, yet God feeds them. And how much more valuable you are than birds! Who of you by worrying can add a single hour to his life? Since you cannot do this very little thing, why do you worry about the rest?"

Mentally, I began to wonder if I needed the bedtime anxiety medication anymore. My anxiety had become non-existent. I lost the stress and the need to want to control everything all the time. I was convinced, I was heavenly guided, everything was happening for a reason, and all was well in the moment. The new felt self-love had me respecting myself and my time.

It was August 2017. Al picked up our prescriptions from the pharmacy. His prescription comes in a square box. Mine would be a small bottle. The little white paper sack they came in sat on top of the kitchen island.

The medication box it had held kept the sack in an expanded, open look. The box was not sticking out of the sack, which told me it was put away. I assumed all the medications had been removed, and the sack was empty, but had not made it to the trash can yet. I picked it up, without looking in it, and threw it away.

Two days later, I couldn't find my bottle of medication—one of the few medications I continued to have on hand. I assumed Al picked it up along with his that day. It was the anxiety medication I take at bedtime and or flying/road trips. I was confident I called it in with his.

I questioned him later on if he picked them up. He thought so. He wasn't sure. I looked again next to the refrigerator, which is where they may have been placed. They weren't there. I recalled throwing the sack away that day. Besides the batch of paperwork stapled to the outside, it felt empty.

But now I wonder if the bottle was in it. I called the pharmacy to see if, indeed, he received the prescription. He had; a 3-month supply. I was told they could not refill it, in light of its disappearance, or dis-guarded mishap.

Trash day was the day before, meaning the trash bag with the white thrown away prescription sack went with it. There went my pills. I guess it was my sign. I no longer needed the prescription drug to sleep, or for any other reason. After many years of taking them, the need was gone.

MAGIC ANSWER

The side-effects had taunted me. It was the third, or maybe fourth, antidepressant medication I'd try over the extended years. The first one, many moons ago, affected the muscles in my left arm, leaving me unable to lift it. Two others along the way kept me from sleeping, even with my nighttime anxiety pill used for sleeping.

This one, I started in 2008. It was a newly released drug, with hopes it might help my esophageal spasms, IBS, anxiety, and symptoms. After two months of the low dosage, with no relief, the dose was increased.

An annoying and nagging pain in the middle of my forehead after that had me believing I had a sinus infection. My sinuses were x-rayed three different times. Each time, the results were negative. I, nor my physician, would attribute it to being a side-effect of the newest antidepressant.

Then there were times of dizziness when arising in the mornings. As I sat and rose to get out of bed, my head spun. The room spun, and the only thing I could do was lay directly back down. I would call in sick to work, left to battle the dizziness, lying in bed.

In September 2011, I correlated together the dizziness episode with a missed dose of the antidepressant. I was not one to inadvertently miss a dosage, but there were a few times I would be out, and the refill had not gotten picked up.

With a recent morning dizzy episode, and a missed dose, my mind told me the dizziness occurrences might be from the missed dose. I'd missed my morning dose the day before, waiting on pickup. With this correlation and thought, I desired not to take them any longer. If missing a dosage could cause that much distress, was it worth taking?

I slowly weaned myself off the antidepressant. The last month to take them would be October 2011. My benzodiazepine anxiety medication was switched with an anxiolytic anxiety medication. To be taken twice daily.

Here the tingling and numbness in my hands, along with headaches, left me again, not wanting to take the newest drug. I discontinued this medicine and went back on my original anxiety medication (the one recently thrown out).

Over the next six months, without the antidepressant, I was doing well, I thought. My IBS though, showed me differently. I found myself on a slippery slope. Without symptoms or warning, and in a moment's notice, a restroom was needed.

It could happen at any moment; that moment was never a good moment. Time to make it to the restroom, in an instant moment's notice, was impossible. Here, I found myself in uncontrollable, undesirable, unwanted situations.

Life…in truth, had taken another fricking "shitty" wrong turn. The thought of wearing a diaper, or a colostomy bag, was haunting.

In January 2012, my office visit stated: "struggling with anxiety. She wishes to speak of alternative, all-natural products sold to help with anxiety. Due to her symptoms,

I feel these would be ineffective, especially for the significance of her symptoms of 'restlessness, anxiety, and mild depression'.

She describes being restless, not eating, anxious, poor concentration. Off-the-wall anxiety. Her symptoms have been exacerbated with the death of a 3-week old baby of her niece, and her uncle dying. She also helped take her father to the ER. All in the last two weeks."

My doctor recommended another antidepressant, along with the possibility of a psychiatric consult for psychopharmacological management (whatever that was). If symptoms proved challenging to control. A new prescription for another antidepressant was written, filled, and started.

A follow up was in early April 2012. The office note read, "Nobody will have a magic answer for her. IBS has often flared with increased stress; level has been so so lately. She also had another episode where she could not make it to the toilet. Has been taking her IBS medication, with little results."

He requested another colonoscopy, my favorite thing to do. As was routine for me, I did it again. I passed out doing the cleanout prep the night before. A polyp was found and removed in the procedure. Otherwise, it was negative for any other disease or diagnosis.

On April 30, 2012, my brother Ron passed away from heart disease.

It was December 3, 2012. Awakened in the middle of the night with the lower abdominal cramping pain that came with the IBS, I arose from bed and walked to the kitchen looking for something to drink. Hoping to settle the symptoms.

Afterwards, returning to the bedroom, I felt myself getting lightheaded. The next thing I recall is, yelling for Al. I was lying on the floor, at the bottom of the 12 stairs leading to the basement. My skin is sweaty, clammy, and moist. I was in a daze.

I let out a weak call for Al; I'm not sure how he heard me. He found me and rounded up Colton, who was in his bedroom, still up. They helped me up the stairway and back to bed.

Two days later, I saw my physician. In the fall, I sustained a contusion at the base of my neck, my right side, and shoulder. My tailbone was sore as well. My blood pressure was elevated; 156/94, supine-190/120, standing 170/80, and later, 150/110. Blood pressure medication was prescribed.

At my next annual appointment, in May 2013, my BP was still elevated 152/92. My complaint was the spastic esophagus pain. A proton-pump inhibitor (acid reflux medication) was prescribed.

I didn't see my physician again, until my next annual exam, in May 2014. At this time, I stated the spastic esophagus was bothering me more than the IBS. It was primarily a squeezing and pressure in my upper abdomen and my back. The acid reflux medication wasn't a big help.

My blood pressure continued to be elevated from 140/93, 152/99, to 160/112. The BP medication dosage was increased, and a diuretic and potassium were prescribed. The antidepressant was also increased to 40 mg.

My anxiety, along with the IBS, and esophageal spasms, was causing hypertension. With all my pain and worries in health, it was taking me towards a hazardous, cardiovascular road.

On January 27, 2015, my brother Lenny took his life.

I wouldn't see my physician until June 2015. Five months after Lenny's suicide. Clyde had passed away a couple of weeks earlier. The office note stated, "she did extremely well, as far as her IBS and anxiety during this time.

Between her faith and family, she has gotten by pretty well with no major upset. She is having occasional hot flashes and night sweats. BP is controlled at home, but high here. Thyroid was over suppressed, and the hormone dosage will be decreased from 125mg to 100mg."

In September 2015. I was introduced to the chakras and life's energy. I immediately began researching, reading, learning of the spiritual energy centers within us. A source I had no idea existed. I took part in the process of letting go and forgiving. And with it, I was releasing stuck lower negative energy inside.

My lower abdominal cramping episodes, bloating, mishaps, and symptoms from the IBS were no longer present. By the end of 2015, four-months later, the IBS medication was not being used. After 32 years, the undesirable symptoms were gone.

The Proton Inhibitor for my upper gut pain was also discontinued. I hadn't had any upper gut pain or extreme spasm episodes. Besides the spasms it used to be, when I stretched my arms into the air, reaching upward, I would experience a "pressure or knot" feeling in the upper gut area.

This was the area of dominant pain from the very beginning years ago. That feeling was now gone as well. I no longer felt a source of "something-ness." I discontinued the proton inhibitor medication. After 36 years, the gut pain was gone.

At my next appointment in August 2016, the notes stated anxiety generally doing better. "More calm after the death of her brother from suicide in 2015. More spiritual. Has cut antidepressant in half, no GI meds needed. Sleep is not good; hot flashes, no dreams. Will cut down diuretic med due to light-headedness getting up and down."

I would wean myself off the added blood pressure medications and diuretic. BP's ranged from 102/61 to 122/72. I stayed on a low dose of BP med due to having one kidney. The need for potassium was also no longer needed. My anxiety was calming and controlled, alleviating hypertension. I began to lower the antidepressant dosages, little by little, as well.

A follow-up appointment was in April 2017. Records state she is doing well, no concerns. Feels her anxiety is much better, controlling her symptoms. She has been working on relaxation and meditation techniques, which she feels like she is doing much better with her spiritual stuff—wonders about lowering antidepressants from 20mg to 10mg.

In my annual physical in November 2017, the diagnosis read: "anxiety resolved, depressive disorder, recurrent, in FULL remission; IBS resolved, hypertension controlled. Hypothyroid, controlled".

It took me time to stop the antidepressant altogether. Memories of what had occurred when I quit them in 2012 kept me guarded. I slowly lowered the dosage to 5 mg, and in April 2018, I discontinued it altogether.

The upper gut pain, dating back to 1979, continuing through life, with a surgery in 2001, exacerbating the problem into esophageal spasms, was gone. The IBS, which dated back to 1983, was resolved. My anxiety was resolved. The depressive recurrent disorder was in *full* remission.

Now, after all these years, I found the magic answer to my health, in which I had no idea existed. I also found what needed to change—my internal energy. It was the magic answer.

CHA…CHA…CHAKRA

We were both laughing out loud. In my visit with Father, his attempts in saying the word were unsuccessful. Each try brought laughter to both our existence. In the end, I repeated the word chakra, one more time for him.

It took me to when I first heard the word too. My reaction was about the same. I wasn't sure what the advisor said in her story and pronunciation. As my research and learning expanded, I found the chakras are the spiritual meridian points in the body. They are called energy centers.

Many books and online resources are available on the chakra system, all defining the seven main chakras as beginning at the tailbone (coccyx), running up the spine and vertebrae, into the top of the head.

Chakra is a Sanskrit word, meaning "Wheel" or "Vortex." Each chakra is a circular ball of energy. Each designated with a specific color. They are said to be related to the bodies' major Endocrine Glands, nervous system, and spiritual, "spirit" energy, within oneself. They are also associated with the lotus flower.

The first chakra is known as the root chakra. It's at the base of the spine and is associated with being grounded. When weak, blocked, or ungrounded, holding low emotional energy, we may experience fear, a lack of self-worth, survival, and financial worries. This lower energy is stored in emotions of safety and security.

I found it stated that if weak, blocked, or deficient, it can be related to many disorders, including colitis, addictions, back pain, stomach problems, depression, low self-esteem, and negative thinking.

The root chakra is said to be jeopardized in our childhood days between birth and the age of seven, when our innocence is trained by our family, daycare providers, teachings, surroundings, and society. I didn't have to look far to know this chakra was off.

Each chakra is associated with a color, non-coincidentally, the same seven colors as the rainbow; the rainbow color associated with the root chakra energy is red. These colors can help in balancing your energy. Merely wearing a colored shirt of the chakra (in this case, red) can assist in aligning and grounding to that particular chakra.

The second chakra, the Sacral chakra, is in the lower abdomen. It is below the belly button and is associated with emotions, feelings, creativity, pleasure, sexual sensations, and enjoyment.

If weak, one may experience reproductive disorders, sexual dysfunction, menstrual difficulties, or bladder and kidney problems. Also included are irritable bowel, and muscle spasms. My held emotions and feelings, along with my chronic illnesses in my deformed kidney and irritable bowel syndrome, would have both the first and second chakras imbalanced. The rainbow color of the sacral chakra energy is orange.

The third chakra, called the solar plexus, is below the sternum in the stomach's pit. It is associated with the Adrenal gland and Pancreas. When not in balance, it is said it can cause digestive issues, ulcers, liver, gallbladder, pancreas, and diabetes problems.

Here it is our emotions of acceptance, self-respect, and self-compassion; fear, guilt, rejection, and worry of physical appearance, are also said to affect our third chakra. I found my inner-self in those categories, which would contribute to my upper gut pain and esophageal spasms. The gut pain, I now relate ongoing back to 1979 at age 19, was in this third chakra area.

I would be jeopardized from my fear acquired in my early hospitalization with the kidney infection. It would come from the self-emotions held inside from early childhood, school years, and experiences, causing doubt, guilt, anxiety, and fear. The rainbow color of the solar plexus chakra energy is yellow.

The heart chakra, the 4th chakra, is behind the sternum and associated with the thymus gland and Circulatory System. It's stated to hold our traumatic and painful events, which seems appropriate. Our sadness, heartaches, relationships, jealousies, feelings, anger, bitterness, fear, and loneliness attach here. All connected to the heart and heartbreaks.

Our love often goes freely, unconditionally, to the ones we love; family, spouse, children, grandchildren or friends. Overriding any love deserved for ourselves. Self-love is not taught and rarely learned. Society doesn't teach it, nor does it seem to want to. And, if you're like I was, except for those other "few days," you would say, "of course, I love myself." Agree?

Yet, in reality, we all carry too much within, so many emotions, to truly, fully, unconditionally love ourselves. It's easier to love others, we are too judgmental in ourselves. We don't like this, and we don't like that about ourselves. We are always trying to change us. We never take credit for the way we simply are. Society says you can't be happy with who you are, and with what is your way.

The heart chakra is influenced by the nervous system; the lungs, heart, circulatory system, and arms. Bringing with it diseases such as allergies, asthma, heart disease, lung disease, lymphatic disease, and breast cancer, upper back, arm, and wrist pain. The rainbow color of the heart chakra energy is green.

The fifth chakra is the throat chakra, associated with the thyroid. This gland is said to be connected to our ability to communicate, to speak. It's our voice, our opinions, our words, bringing us our creative side. When its energy is blocked from feelings and suppressed vocal expression, we have a hard time expressing ourselves—taking away our own power to speak our truth.

You've heard, or may have been told, like we were, "children should be seen, and not heard." We got told that, frequently. Maybe you did too. When taught to suppress our voice, to not speak and share our full expressive selves and feelings, it weakens the fifth chakra's energy.

I now understand my grandmother was raised this way. To hold her voice, to not speak outside the boundaries laid before her by her parents and ancestors. This was passed down to her children, my mom. Who therefore passed it down to me, as well as my siblings.

We all grew up, holding our voices, with emotions and freedom being suppressed, in the thyroid. This, depleting us of life's energy, subsequently causing each of us thyroid deficiencies and diseases.

I and my family are indeed the recipient, through genetics, DNA, heredity, and family dysfunction, in acquiring her genes, in suppressed voices, and thyroid disease. These traits passed on through the family tree.

If the 5th chakra is out of balance, the thyroid, an endocrine gland producing hormone, may become dysfunctional, not producing enough hormones. A weak 5th chakra is to be associated with sore throats, colds, and ear infections.

A raspy voice (which is why my thyroid was tested), cold sores, or lip, and tongue issues are on the list as well. Shoulder and neck pain, along with asthma, and bronchitis may occur as well. The rainbow color of the throat chakra energy is blue.

The third eye, the sixth chakra, sometimes called the Brow Chakra, is said to be associated with the Pineal Gland, as well as the Pituitary gland and the Autonomic Nervous System. It is known as the extra, or third eye, one may see in the middle of the forehead, in chakra, Yoga, and meditation photos. It's centered in the middle of the forehead, where the pineal gland is, which is shaped like a pine cone.

The pineal gland produces melatonin, a derived serotonin hormone. When the third eye is open, it is thought, one may "see clearly now." It connects us to intuition and inner knowledge, giving us the ability to see things more openly. It is your knowing and gut feeling.

If the third eye is blocked or energy deficient, you may experience headaches, migraines, sinus conditions, eyes, ears, and nervous and neurological disorders. It is affected by wanting to figure everything in life out; to control everything.

When my sinuses were x-rayed those three times due to my symptoms, it was in this area of the pineal gland. Now, I believe the antidepressant medication was attributing to my symptoms, affecting the pineal gland.

Once I was weaned off the medicine, the symptom went away. The rainbow color of the third eye chakra is indigo.

The 7th chakra is the crown chakra at the top of the head. It's associated with the central nervous system, the pituitary gland, and the hypothalamus. Here the pineal gland is secondary to the pituitary gland. Because of its location, it is closely associated with the brain and the nervous system.

Symptoms for a weakened seventh chakra include depression, mental and learning disabilities. Confusion and fear are mentioned, as well. When in balance, one trusts in their intuition and themselves. The rainbow color of the crown chakra energy is violet.

If the crown chakra and the other six chakra energies are open and aligned, it is said one may experience what is called a kundalini awakening. This allows one to come closer to their higher self, in enlightenment, and spirituality. Yogi's are known for kundalini awakenings.

The kundalini is to be a form of divine energy, coiled like a snake, or serpent, which travels up from the root chakra at the base of the spine, to the crown chakra on the top of the head. It's said, when the energy flows freely through the seven chakras, it's a path to the oneness of self, happiness, good health, and spiritual awareness and alignment.

The symbol of the kundalini awakening is portrayed as two snakes or serpents, coiled up the spine, entwined with the chakra centers. Interestingly, in the medical field, the staff symbol is represented by two snakes, coiled up the staff. This medical emblem is centuries old.

I also found some religious staff adorn the snake/serpent as well. In a search for the definition of the snake in religion, Wikipedia brings you to serpent, stating they (both) represent fertility or a creative life force, as they shed their skin and are symbols of rebirth, transformation, immortality, and healing.

A search of serpents in the Bible brought up Wikipedia, stating, "the serpent, or snake, is a symbol of evil power, and chaos from the underworld, as well as a symbol of fertility, life, and healing. It is also associated with divination, including the verb form meaning-to practice divination or fortune-telling."

From here, I was taken to an article on the Audience Hall of the Vatican, in Rome. The article spoke of and showed photos of the Pope's Audience Hall. The lecture hall stage within portrays that of a serpent's, or snake's, mouth. As the Pope himself speaks, from the center stage of the Audience Hall, as one looks forward, towards him, you find him standing within what appears to look like the mouth of a giant reptile. There are what appears to be two fangs, hanging down, as well as reptile eyes, which are portrayed on both sides.

My search took me further into the Vatican. I found, inside Vatican City Courtyard, many symbolic pieces of ancient art are displayed. One famously known piece is the Fontana della Pigna. Wikipedia defined the Fontana della Pigna or Pigna ("The Pinecone") as a former Roman fountain that now decorates as a vast niche in the wall of the Vatican, facing the Cortile della Pigna.

The Fountain is composed of a large bronze pine cone, almost four meters high. At one-time water spouted from the top. It's been moved from its original location, twice. It was originally placed near the Pantheon' next to the Temple of Isis, and later moved to its present location within Vatican City in1608.

I could not find a biblical meaning, or purpose, of the pine cone statue within the Vatican City. I did find information on Ancient Symbol's meanings on www.ancient-symbols.com.

Here it states, pine cones were considered symbols of fertility by Romans, Greeks, Assyrians, and Christians. Their design forms a perfect Fibonacci sequence. Pine cones have also been associated with the Third Eye, enlightenment, and the pineal gland.

Ancient civilizations used the pine cone in architecture, sculpture, and paintings. The staff of Osiris has a pinecone on top of two intertwined serpents. Hindu gods have pine cones in their hands. Shiva's hair is woven with snakes in the shape of a pine cone.

Using the pine cones with serpents represents spiritual consciousness. Pine cones have also been used to symbolize eternal life. The Assyrians show a pine cone being used to fertilize the Tree of Life. It has the shape of a pinecone and is located in the brain. The pineal gland regulates melatonin.

The pineal gland, aka the Third Eye, is the intuitive center of the brain. Pinecones have been shown to be atop the staff on the Pope's sacred papal. The staff has been said to represent the spine, with the pinecone representing the pineal gland. Some will say the third eye is mentioned in Matthew 6:22 when Jesus says, "Your eye is like a lamp that provides light for your body. When your eye is healthy, your whole body is filled with light."

Notably, are similarities of the snake/serpent in the chakra system, the ancient medical symbol, and religion. Also noted is a pinecone shaped emblem at the top of religious staffs. I also found a stated correlation of the death of Jesus, at age 33, to the number of vertebrae of a human being, at 33.

Together it's stated it is the symbolization that if the energy rising up the 33 vertebrae flows freely through the energy points (chakras) and endocrine system, up to the pineal gland, this is where Christ consciousness dwells.

When life energy flows freely up the vertebrates, without emotional blocks, one may obtain a higher consciousness, awareness, and wellness.

When the "totem of souls" appeared, it led me to any answers of explanation, reasoning, or meaning I could find. Without answers from numerous sources I reached out to, I was taken to step outside my box, outside my comfort zone, seeking a spiritual advisor. Here, through her, I found a truth and learned of the hidden, healing, spiritual, cha…cha…chakras. This had me dancing, a new step.

IT'S THE LAW!

We live in a world of laws. Laws, laws, laws…to abide by. But not all laws are laws in the legal or judicial, Rule of Law, aspect of society and life. There are laws of many orientations.

The Universe and Science have Laws; there is the Law of Nature, the Law of PI, the Laws of Science, Humanity, Quantum Physics, and Mechanics. We have Newton's Law of Gravity, Duality, Spiritual Laws, and the Law of Kinetic Energy.

There are God's laws, in The 10 Commandments, Laws of Numbers, the Law of Life, and Land. There are law's in every aspect of life, faith, the Universe, and galaxy; too many to comprehend, i.e., mind-boggling. It is up to us to learn the knowledge of those laws, and the benefits of abiding by them, and the repercussions, if not.

In the language of the Universe, there are Universal Spiritual Laws. One is the Law of Attraction. This is where what we think, and believe, is what we receive. Wherein, drawing the same like energies to us. Positive attracts positive; negative attracts negative—simple science.

Within this energy we may control life, to a degree, in our thoughts, in a positive manner, or negative manner. In wellness, or sickness. In happiness or sadness. Here one may change their life energy. Because here is where you attract, what you think, and focus on.

This takes us to the Law of Vibration. Here, it states everything carries vibration to it; our actions, our voices, decisions, and life choices. Every choice and decision is a vibration in energy, stated to be felt in Heaven and the Universe.

The negative energies, weigh on our minds, bodies, health, and livelihood; the positive energy bringing happiness, joy, peace, good health, and gratitude. It's in our choices, our words, and our thoughts and actions, in which we may find grace or illness.

The Law of Cause and Effect says that events don't happen coincidentally. There are no coincidences; everything happens for a reason, no matter if you see how or why it happened. It can be related to the concept of karma. We cannot plant seeds of poor decisions and reap a harvest of goodwill.

The Law of Compensation is like an extension of the Law of Cause and Effect, meaning what is put out is what is given back in abundance. If you do good deeds and share kindness, you'll receive good things back. The same goes for negative and greedy actions.

The Law of Correspondence, states "as above, so below." This means whatever happens inside your mental space is reflected on the outside. This states that what you think, see, and feel in your conscious and subconscious mind is what you create on the outside.

The Law of Energy states everything is made of energy. It goes with the Law of Vibration, meaning that energy comes in countless frequency levels, and is being sent out to the Universe constantly, in which the law of energy is always in motion.

There is also the law of Perpetual Transmutation of Energy. This means you have the ability to change your life into anything you want. It's your responsibility to transform your life energy, and it's your choice to accept or reject the opportunities that the Universe gives you.

This law is where I had a choice. God and the Universe were giving me all the signs and messages to find and transform my life. Yet, it was up to me to follow. I had free will. To continue on the path.

Nikola Tesla, a famous scientist, quoted and declared, "If you want to find the secrets of the Universe, think in terms of energy, frequency, and vibration; the whole of the Universe is energy, and each basic element of the known atomic chart consists of energy at different rates of vibration."

This energy is a frequency or vibration; each individual can learn to utilize this energy for spiritual growth and constructive purposes. It raises the level of consciousness of man, and in turn, raises his/her vibration or vibes.

Each person has a different vibration. Each person's earthly actions are created by his thought projections. What we've experienced is projected into our mind, in thoughts. In spiritual growth, one works to eliminate and accept negative thoughts. Knowing those thoughts weigh on our bodies and create reality. Here one grows both physically and spiritually. This is the Universal Energy of Vibrations.

Nikola Tesla declared the concept that "everything, whether human, plant, animals, or rocks, provided certain forms of energy, they can alter the vibrational resonance of other forms of energy." This is said to be why healing crystals and stones are still used today. They can alter your vibration positively.

Albert Einstein also stated everything in life is a vibration. The Universal Law of Nature states everything has its own vibration-it goes with basic chemistry in which everything is made up of atoms. These atoms can be as a solid, liquid, or gas. All with their own vibrations, every sound, thought, and feeling is a vibration.

The Law of Vibration serves as the foundation for the Law of Attraction, which takes us to manifestation. Together, our energy and vibrations create the Law of Attraction, i.e., LOA. Bringing one to manifest, through manifestation. To create, with our thoughts.

THE VINTAGE DESK

I saw it for sale online in the marketplace. We'd looked at them multiple times at sales and auctions, but never purchased one. When I saw it that day, I didn't pay attention to the material looks, as I knew I would be refurbishing it if I purchased it. It was $25, and would be a fun little project.

Plus, the other L-shaped desk I arranged in the living room wasn't working out so well. I thought maybe I could use this. My laptop could fit on top nicely. I sent a message through the website, asking if it was still available. I received a response shortly thereafter stating it was.

Pickup was outside a small neighboring town, approximately 30-miles East of home. As luck was on my side, we would be driving through there on Friday.

My birthday was Friday. Time moves steadily forward. We'd made plans to celebrate it at the Casino by Topeka, playing Bingo. We would be driving through her town, on our way, and could easily stop and pick up the vintage wood and metal school desk.

We left the house around 4:00 p.m. with arrangements pre-made to pick the desk up around 4:30 p.m. We traveled the 30-minute drive through the small towns along Hwy 24. We had MapQuest on. Arriving in our designated town, a few blocks down the main street, the voice on my phone spoke. We would need to take a left at the next intersection.

It was roughly 5-miles out of town. Located in a subdivision of homes. The pebble rocked driveway was off the main road. We pulled in, parked close to the house, and exited the vehicle. I went to the front door and rang the doorbell. Al stood outside at the truck.

An elderly woman answered the door, letting me inside. The desk was sitting off the side of the front door. We stepped over towards it. In seeing it, and the marks and drawings on the top, I was awestruck.

The top of the desk displayed pencil, hand-drawn pictures. A partial circle is in the middle of the wooden top. In the middle of the circle is what appears to be an eye. A third eye? Drawn off to the outside of the partial circle are hand-drawn male and female figures.

I am surprised. My mind says, "of course this desk was for me." It displayed what I would say is a third eye, the 6th chakra representation. Also drawn, and displayed, are a boy and girl. This could be displaying the feminine and masculine identity, which is another theory factor in life I was learning about.

Now, I had a desk, portraying the same. I didn't hesitate. I told the women I would take it, handing her my cash. I walked back to the front door, calling outside to Al to come help get the desk.

Initially seeing it, he commented it "was a great buy." As we loaded it onto the bed of the truck, I pointed out the top and the drawings on it. He said, "yes, it would sand off nicely."
But…wait! Sand…sand off the top? Sand off the ancient drawings. Something a child drew years ago, relating to what I believe is the 3rd eye—the mere thing I was aligning with.

There were also the two drawn people on it. Those drawings could be showing the connection between the feminine and masculine identities.

When I saw it online that day, my intentions were to refurbish it. To sand it down. I didn't look at the photos closely, knowing that's what I would be doing. That's what I love to do. This, more often than not, requires sanding, and staining, or painting. But now, with what I see, I'm not sure I can do that, to this.

I spent the next week working on the desk. I did some light hand sanding on the top and around the inner "artistic" drawings; I didn't touch them. I then touched it up with a light oak stain. Al cut two boards to attach the bottom legs on. It would stabilize the seat and allow the seat to be placed farther back. Without that, I fit, but it was a tight fit. A few more inches between the desk, and the seat, would help.

Once finished, we moved it inside to the living room area. I would experiment with it in another writing workspace. The make-shift desk set-up in the living room didn't work out like I had hoped. It was awkward, had no back support, or comfort.

WORD!

It took me time to understand; truthfully, it took me a long time to get it. I had a hunch, in the appearance of St. Peter, but it was the sculptured artwork I miraculously painted on the paper plate, in which I began to put the pieces together.

In my discovery, I began to ask people about "this" particular word I related to my findings. Here, I discovered, no one could or would, in the moment, define, or give me an example of it. They could not relate it to something.

This word, with an unknown identification, undefined knowing, meaning, or action, manifest. Dictionary.com defines manifest as; "1. readily perceived by the eye or the understanding; evident; obvious; apparent; plain. 2. Psychoanalysis of or relating to conscious feelings, ideas, and impulses that contain repressed psychic material. 3. To make clear or evident to the eye or the understanding; show plainly. 4. To prove; put beyond doubt or question."

In scripture, we can find manifest and meanings in the following:

• "For there is nothing hidden which shall not be made manifest; nor does any secret thing take place, but that it should come to light." Mrk 4:22
• "This was now the third time that Jesus revealed Himself (appeared, was manifest) to the disciples after He had risen from the dead." John 21:14
• "To each person has been given the ability to manifest the Spirit for the common good." 1 Cor 12:7
• "Whatever you ask for in prayer, believe that you have received it, and it will be yours." Mark 11:24

Manifest, then takes us to manifestation. Vocabulary.com defines it as "a manifestation is the public display of emotion, or feeling, or something theoretical made real." Manifestation is where dreams become real. Our thoughts, and belief in something, becomes a reality. What we think we put into manifestation. What we believe in comes to light.

In receiving the "Flowers from Heaven," that day, I believed, in my heart, it was my sign of my brother's eternal life. The sign I petitioned for. Now, I believe my belief in receiving the eternal life-sign gave way for the manifestation of the physical "totem of souls."

In believing I'd received my sign, through my mind, and emotional energy, it manifested into a visible symbol. I had compiled the energy, along with the vibration, producing the amazing form out of ashes. I manifested what my mind and soul portrayed as a visual eternal life sign.

The same can be said of St. Peter. In receiving the letter that day, with his name on it, as well as searching him out, it gave way to the energy of portraying him. In my mind and subconscious, the energy and vibration manifested into his appearance.

In my patio furniture refurbishing, thoughts and energy were on my brother Lenny. Then, I painted him. As I did the touch-up, with the small artist paintbrush, I artistically, unknowingly, painted a side view sculpture of him, through my mental energy and vibrations.

And most recently, the vintage school desk. With my energy, vibrations (vibes), and constant thought and awareness of the chakras, along with the pineal gland and the third eye, the desk appears. My energetic thoughts aligned me with the desk. It's phenomenally astonishing.

For me, prior to this, the words manifest, and manifestation, I related to cancer. Hearing of people's diagnoses of cancer manifesting to other parts of the body, growing, spreading. My mind never took it to the fact that I or you are making things happen, by thought, through manifestation, into reality.

I'd never been subjected to this knowledge. I never related what I did, or what I thought, into bringing something into existence, making something happen or appear. Where things are brought into reality by thinking, thought, energy, and belief. Where thoughts turn into things, is not taught.

The next word I was led to was The Word of Knowledge. The Word of Knowledge, in Christianity, is a spiritual gift listed in Corinthians 12:8, "For to one is given by the Spirit the word of wisdom; to another the word of knowledge by the same Spirit."

It is written the Word of Knowledge is associated with the ability to teach the faith, but also with attributes to revelation, similar to prophecy. It is a revelation because God is revealing something to you. The Holy Spirit is relaying a specific message and knowledge one would not normally know.

It is closely related to the spiritual word and gift, The Word of Wisdom. For what good would it be to learn something of knowledge, and not have the wisdom to know what to do with it. Knowledge is no good if you don't have the wisdom to share.

Here I looked to the Word of Knowledge in the revelations revealed to me. I looked to the Word of Wisdom, knowing faith and spirit had guided me. And the difficult task became easier. I needed to share my new inner guidance, faith, healing, and findings of the magnitude of a single, defined word.

A simple word, unbeknownst to most, for its dynamic power. A word whose actions lead us on the roadmap of life; in its peaks and valleys; in happiness, and sadness, and in love and hate; in emotions. This word is manifest.

ONE LIFE, MANY NAMES

Life can come with an array of different names. Besides our birth name, we may acquire nicknames, professional names, stage names, handle's, and aliases. Names we've given ourselves, or given by someone else, it represents us in some way.

This nickname is generally due to a personality, trait, hobby, career, business, or some other characteristic notion or wits.

As I went down life's memory lane, it brought me to more than one name I either was given by someone, by myself, or I myself gave to something. It was fascinating, aligning them to life. My first memory nickname, as you may know, was the nickname "skinny."

****

It was a 1970's dark blue Ford F-150 pickup. The tires are super heavy-duty, setting it up high from the ground. The stereo system was of Bose quality and blared your favorite song as you drove proudly down the road.

Under the dash was an installed CB radio. A white-coated antenna was attached to the top of the truck for the reception. It was a hot, sporty, attractive looking truck.

Breaker, breaker, good buddy. Do you copy? 10-4 (yes, I copy). What's your 10-2 (location)? Headed North on Highway 183 at yardstick (Mile Marker) 5. Ten-4 good buddy. My bird dog (radar detector) sensed a smoky bear (police) at yardstick 10. It's a clean shot (no cops) ahead after that, to put the hammer down (excel speed).

Daddy was a CB radioman. The square boxed communication devices were in all locations, the bar, home, and in the vehicle. The vehicle above. As a young teenager, I didn't get to drive the truck much. But when I did, I took complete advantage of it, utilizing the CB communication device.

Throughout my teenage years, I worked for my parents who owned a restaurant, lounge, and bowling alley. The restaurant was open Thursday, Friday, and Saturday nights. I waited tables. No, not the greatest hours for a teenager.

Yet, us girls, my sisters and I, we had to do it. It was a family business. It was also spending and gas money.

There were basketball games, football games, Friday night dances, and then the dragging of the main street. In our growing up days of small-town living, dragging main was the number one thing to do.

If you were not at a school function or in a vehicle dragging main, you were parked on one of the store parking lots, along with a congregation of other vehicles and people.

The restaurant closed at 11:00 p.m. on Friday and Saturday nights. Making it 11:30 p.m. before I was off work. Maybe later if it was busy. Therefore, my time of dragging the mile-long main street, or parking in the main street lots, in our small little town, was more in the midnight hour.

In giving myself a CB handle name, for when I did get to drive the truck, I chose the "Midnight Rider." Coming from the popular 1970's song, The Midnight Rider, by The Allman Brothers. It seemed appropriate.

****

Our phone rang. It was my brother. He was in a pickle and needed help. I relayed the message to Al. It would take a trip to Wichita, but we would head that way to help him out.

Our phone rang. It was my other brother. He needed medical advice on the health issues he was having. With my dental and oral surgery training, and work, came the necessity to learn the medical side as well. I could help answer some of his questions.

Our phone rang. It was another brother. My nephew was in a bad car accident and was in the hospital; he needed advice. Working in the insurance and legal field, I acquired knowledgeable experience and was able to help guide him through the process.

Our phone rang. It was my youngest brother. He couldn't understand why mother wouldn't let him do things on his own. I'd tell him he was her baby, and special. And because she only wanted what was best for him. He was her youngest and handicapped. She would always care for his best interests.

Our phone rang...it was my sisters…over and over through the years I was my family's go-to person. So much so that after time, Al began to call me the Godmother. My family needed help and assistance. I would answer their call. Of course, most often, with his help.

While a godmother in the Christian faith is a woman who chooses to take on a child's life responsibilities if their parents pass, it was my family's continued callings, and my guidance, in which Al placed the Godmother nickname upon me.

As we would jokingly laugh about it, it was funny, because I was in a way, God-motherly guidance to them. Helping them weave their way through some of their own difficult roads. And in truth, I wouldn't have wanted it any other way.

****

Twitter! Yep. You've heard of it, right? With the political arena today, Twitter has become a known talking point.

In 2011, prior to either of my brother's passing, I decided to open a twitter account. So many talked about it. I could keep up with sports and the K-State Wildcats with it.

It was Saturday afternoon. I was at the desk in the office setting up the new account. I set up the password. Next was the option to add the account name. I'd been sitting for a few minutes, thinking. Do I just use my name, or go with something different? What name did I want to use?

Al knew I was setting up the account. He poked his head into the office on his way to the restroom. I jokingly asked his opinion on what I should use for my account name. He laughed, of course, saying, "I don't know." As he turned to leave, my fingers began to type.

Turning back around, he asked, "what did you go with?" Looking at him, I proudly relayed, "magicladi." He laughed-out-loud, asking me why. Why would I choose such a name?

I laughed too and shrugged my shoulders. "I wasn't specifically sure," I replied. It appeared in my mind, in that instant, and that's what I went with. In the twitter world, I was now the "magicladi."

****

I found him in the newspaper for sale. My sister-in-law and I took the short drive to the country to see him. As you may understand, one does not go to look at a new puppy without going home with it. We left with him. He was adorable. He carried a sophisticated look, to me.

Naming a dog can be easy or hard. You look at it, and its characters, and look to come up with a matching name that resonates.

This dog, the puppy, came with a masterful, prestigious look in my eyes. In my mind, Shakespeare spoke to me.

It took me a while to convince the family of the name. They thought it was stupid. Rightfully so, I guess. But I wasn't giving in for some reason. The name stayed. In time, he too, was given a nickname. He became Shaky.

My poem, "Gone into the Night," is in his memory. As I've gone back, I am taken to why a girl who has read not a pinch of Shakespeare that she can remember, comes up with that name for their pet. Besides being guided by that inner voice, the spirit guide, in her head.

Now, I had to research him. To find out a bit more about him. Shakespeare was a writer and poet. That I knew. But that's about all I knew. Wikipedia stated him to be known as the greatest writer and poet in the English language.

He was a play writer, writing Romeo and Juliet as well as numerous other plays. Interestingly, I found many of the characters in his love story plays were known to have taken their own life, suicide.

A MESSAGE, NOT IN A BOTTLE

Love. It's why I am here. It's what brought me to this moment. The love for a brother, whom I lost. That love, which would never be felt or shared together, here, again. But as I've found, love never ends. He is closer to me now than ever before. I just can't physically see him.

This morning, while online, I came across a post shared on another site where people share signs from their loved ones. The sign in this post was a large, perfectly shaped, white cloud heart, in the open blue sky. My mind said it was the most perfect, beautiful sign of love from the other side. I shared it with my *Signs for my Soul* page saying so.

Late afternoon, I went out back. Outdoors, to feed the birds and squirrels. I would also water the newly planted grass, which we planted in the area of the now gone portable pool area. I went to the side of the house to retrieve the water hose.

As I approached closer to the side of the house, I was drawn to a small piece of paper in the yard. It's lying next to the window well—the only piece of paper on the ground. I walked over to pick it up to throw away.

I see the piece of paper is from a small spiral notebook. My mind spoke, wondering if it had something on it. My inner voice says it may be a message. Like a message in the bottle, as I laughed to myself at my crazy thought. I reached down and picked it up.

Unfolding it, I see it is written on. I also see what is written. It "is" a message, an amazing message, at that. Seeing what it said, my heart was thumping at a rapid pace. It outdid the heart in the sky I'd seen and shared earlier.

It wasn't a message in a bottle, which is where my mind jokingly swayed earlier. But it was a wondrous message—a definitive message of love. On the small piece of paper was a penciled, handwritten message, portraying "I ♥ U."

I was smiling in happiness. I almost chuckled, thinking of my brother(s). It was just like them, to want to outdo the cloud heart in the sky sign. They couldn't let me believe that was the most beautiful sign of love from the other side. They had to give me something better, and this one was mine.

How powerful love is. It never dies. It transforms. It is the essence of life, energy, spirit, and soul. God is unconditional love; there is only love when we leave here. On earth, He wills us to become and give His love. And if we are open to it, we may find love can be found in and around us, everywhere.

THE WATER PITCHER

It was an estate sale, in which I found and purchased the water pitcher. The photographic design on the porcelain pitcher caught my eye. It portrayed a tree—limbs reaching out into the sky. In the middle is a roundness of bark, forming a head with facial recognition. It reminded me of what I saw in my trash can.

The human body form, made of ashes, forming what appears to be feet, legs, a waist with breasts, and arms. The arms reaching into the sky. The same as the tree branches on the figurine in the water pitcher. It gave the look of a human tree.

When home, I looked at them in unison. Here, my higher-self spoke of the tree of life. It seems no coincidence I was placed in the path of the pitcher. It would bring me back to the Tree of Life, to where my education and healing began.

In the Book of Genesis, Chapter 2, verse 9, the tree of life is described as being "in the midst of the Garden of Eden with the tree of the knowledge of good and evil. After the fall of man, lest he put forth his hand, and also take of the tree of life and eat, and live forever."

The Tree of Life is said to be a symbol of new beginnings, positive energy, good health, and abundance. As the tree grows in age, it becomes immortal, bearing seeds of future growth. In my theory, humans are the seeds, sown, and nurtured from the ancestral tree of life.

While I can't identify any particular subject in the totem, one identification that speaks to me is they may be ancestors. My request was a sign of the eternal life of a family member. Leaving open a possibility, the unidentified are the life-line of those in eternal life; my eternal family and ancestors—the life-line of loved ones, whose spirits energy dwell in eternity.

The same ancestors, whose traits, genetics, DNA, and heredities, transferred down through the family tree. The same entities I loved dearly, but also was forgiving in heredity, for personalities, and wellness, that weren't mine.

Spirituality says family dysfunction rolls down from generation to generation, like an out of control vehicle on a wet, slippery, muddy road. This takes the entire bloodline down the same paths until one person has the courage to turn and face the flames. This person will bring change to generations that follow.

Yet, these same identities throughout the bloodline are said to be our loved ones in spirit cheering us on, guiding us, in removing the ancestry family plaques. They followed them as well; they too, want the "buck to stop here."

A water pitcher is a device used for watering. It brings cleanliness and freshness, along with nurturing and growth. While I see no coincidence of it in my path, in helping identify the totem of souls, I was also taken to the thought of its use; watering.

Water is essential in growth. All entities require water to survive. To grow, sprout, flourish, and blossom. If we don't water our plants, crops, or grass, they will not grow. And I can't help but think how true this is in life.

Every day we are given the opportunity to water, grow, and cultivate ourselves. This may require the removing of old, decayed branches and bark (forgiveness). We may need to rake the dirt and soil (positive affirmations, prayer, meditate). And in doing so, one can begin to see clarity, in the beauty arising into a new landscape (self-love, wellness and grace).

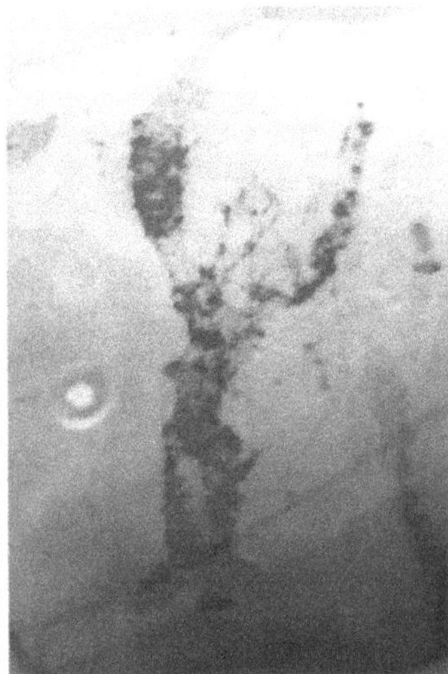

TRUSTING THE PROCESS

If you think about it, each moment we seem to play the odds in life, in what we choose to do, or how we do it, or how we reply to an incident or opportunity. Everything we do is said to be of our own free will. Our own choices and decisions give us free will.

Today's internet access, along with multiple search engines, gives us the opportunity for any amount of information desired, in good, and bad, in truth and falsity. While I was unable to find one person, or an example, to answer the reasons or how's, of the totem of souls, I've got it now—a verdict of sorts.

I created it. I manifested it and St. Peter, along with so many other things. All out of my energetic thoughts. The mind, I've found, is a powerful tool. Manifest and manifestation are key characters. We energetically create with our thoughts. We are co-creators in and through our thoughts and own vibrations.

In my quest, I found the chakra energy therapy consisting of forgiveness, belief, prayer, affirmations and meditation, were all the same things taught in Christianity. I also learned to breathe. To take a breath, and to watch that breath, knowing I was well and guided, in that moment. It appeared I was.

These brought me the lifeline to my remissions. The lifeline of health battles endured was silently diminished, swiftly changing, my inner health, and energy—this, the change I needed.

And I think to myself, had it not been for the totem of souls, I would've not learned of the chakras and all the types of energy healing. I would not have learned of ancient and current Christian history; leaving questions remaining. And I wouldn't have found the magic cure I longed for. I am so thankful and blessed, I kept playing the odds, trusting the process.

It is true you can't see a chakra. It won't show on an X-ray. You won't see it in an MRI or CT scan; or when one is cut open for surgery. They don't exist, to the human eye.

But, research and history show they've been spoken of, and acknowledged, in Christianity, and other religions, beliefs, and practices throughout ancient decades. Mentally, chakras can be envisioned and represented in thought.

The same can be said of God, Jesus, Yahweh, the Universe, or the one you call your higher source creator. Angels, spirit, personal wishes, and dreams are part of thought processes. We cannot see them, yet we can envision them, and believe in their existence.

Science tells us emotions can attach to our physical health, weighing on us and our health/organs. It's now I relate those emotions with negative energy: this energy, causing diseases, health issues, pain, and immune problems.

Many chronic issues I've learned come from our thoughts, experiences, and past memories. Childhood memories are huge. Wherein early childhood experiences are a power, in our inner child, and inner voice.

That voice which speaks to ourselves in judgment, fear, self-worth, and self-confidence. The inner child, from the emotions of childhood experiences. This emotional energy causing the fight to flight response.

The same emotions I now contribute to my anxiety, night sweats, hot flashes, and, consequently, life's health issues. The early kidney hospitalization, having no voice, choice, or control over the painful, horrid daily experiences, left an emotional mark unknowingly within me.

The trauma made way for fear of any and all medical or dental proceedings. The chronic urinary infections thereafter, had my thought energy process in a constant illness frequency.

The name-calling and teasing from the kids, throughout childhood, in my physical skinny bodily appearance, unknowingly left a mark within my subconscious. The emotional feelings of rejection left unknown trauma. All causing havoc to my entire life and health. Who would've imagined that?

Millions of people suffer from anxiety. Anxiety is the most common mental illness in the US. Along with childhood experiences, it's caused by risk factors of genetics, brain chemistry, personality traits, and life events.

All go along with depression, OCD, ADHD, and PTSD. All affecting one's livelihood, life, wellbeing, and health. When coming from childhood, it is known as ACE—Adverse Childhood Experiences.

According to the CDC, ACE is related to traumatic events endured in childhood. Events that caused an emotional experience, pain, or fear. Leaving a mark on the child. It is related to chronic health problems in adulthood, which comes from those childhood experiences. Here, I would find myself a statistic in this diagnosis.

As I continued to trust the process, outside my box, playing the odds, in and through grace, my heart, gut intuition, and faith, I was healing myself. I replaced old negative energy with positive energy.

I came to understand I was never alone. I was perpetually surrounded by the energy of a loved one's spirit, angels, and higher source. Being in the right place at the right time, beyond coincidental.

I knew I wasn't alone in my illnesses. I was like billions of others, battling daily life's anxiety and health issues, many unseen, and often unimaginable. Most, without known chemistry or knowledge to heal the very disease they battle.

While I came to understand the difficult task of getting personal, I also knew I was on a mission. I knew what my heart and soul desired. I knew God and the Universe were supporting me in every way. A specific destination, in purpose, and destiny, per se. And I knew I could not share the rest of this journey, again.

Because I knew, in trusting the process, my story would touch each and every person that reads it. I was in the position, in purpose, to help others. Showing how powerful our very own thoughts are, in what we think, and give energy to—something unknown to most.

I would show how childhood experiences can silently affect our adulthood health. How changing our inner energies and releasing attachments can change and heal our internal and mental wellbeing in body, mind, and spirit; in sickness and health.

And I know the magnitude of hope and healing it can bring to others. A knowledge of life's energetic manifestations and internal healing for those who, like I, never heard of the important spiritual life truths, seemingly suppressed, in time.

LIFE PATH

Time seemingly appeared that I was always in the right place at the right time, on the correct path. As I also went back through life and experiences, I reminisced about the amazingly coincidental names and aliases associated with me. They appeared to align strategically in meaning, for a life path.

For what I found, once upon a time, I was the Midnight Rider. Now I cometh, the Midnight Writer. No longer dragging Main Street in the midnight hour, but writing stories into late-night hours. Expressing words, not in lyrics or song, but writing stories, all night long.

As Shakespeare once said, "To thine own self be true," I now found it fascinating I found my inner self while searching for life's truth. While I can't state why I chose, and demanded, our dog's name as Shakespeare, non-coincidently, we are both poets and writers, in which our writing and work are of Christian character, and whose characters die by suicide.

While Al and I would often laugh at the Godmother nickname, it was true. I was indeed a Godmother, at the time. Those two children have now grown into adults, and I give thanks, I was not called upon to carry out those responsibilities. But in that time, I would take on sisterly cares, family cares, faithful in helping, and assisting, in a God motherly way.

Dictionary.com defines magic as the art of producing illusions as entertainment by the use of sleight of hand. It also states the use of this art: Magic, it was believed, could drive illness from the body.

In what I've learned, I now ponder, did my spirit guide(s), in 2011, guide me to my twitter name, magicladi, knowing my path would have me find the magic within me, four years later? Or by giving myself the name, did it manifest into reality? Bringing me to finding the magic within. It's one or the other.

Then there was my stated purpose in life of paying medical bills in the 1980's. And I think how true that statement and purpose became. If it weren't for that truth, and my chronic health issues and bills, I wouldn't have this miraculous story to tell, in purpose, of God's healing ways. Was this predesigned, as we are told?

I wasn't sure what St. Peter had to do with my journey. What would make spirit draw me to his name? What would make his appearance so worthy? We know St. Peter denied God over and over. Yet God used him in significant ways, knowing Peter could be taught.

Due to his following, God would give St. Peter the name, The Rock. Here, I bring light to this not so easy task, life had given me. Except through awakening, I discovered, life hadn't brought me here, it wasn't in my destiny, or in who I am, to hold on to it.

No, I was a faithful servant, in determination, with answers, in a calling, and a purpose to share. And as hard as the devilish ego side tried, whispering within, I wasn't strong enough, or good enough to complete this task, I softly spoke back.

I am enough, I am a child of God, a warrior, a light-worker, and a Rock, solid in faith and truth, and nobody, will stop the Midnight Writer. She has a vision, and an abundance of other words, to write.

Poetry by Lisa

Falling Star

Once I wished on a falling star
It kept on falling, but never went far
I watched it in the nighttime sky
Swiftly moving, flying high.

Once I wished on a falling star
Maybe it would bring me that brand new car
As it raced through the nighttime air
I could not lose my mesmerizing stare.

Once I wished on a falling star
Hoping it would hear me, off in the far
The magic of the nighttime sky
Took me farther, let me fly!

Now magic has come through
God gave it to me; I am new
Twas, not the falling star I plead
It was magic inside my head.

The Magic Inside

I was blind; I did not see
Life itself was within me
Had He not led me, on the how
My life wouldn't be what it is now.

He takes away with one swift hand
In this life, on this land
We are travelers on this place called earth
God gave us life; He called it birth.

He giveth back, for us to grow
Lessons learned, are what we sow
Life itself is ours, you see
There's magic inside if you believe.

I AM

I am the answers, deep inside
If you let me, I'll be your guide
I will help you understand
Life is yours; make it grand.

I come to you throughout the day
I am the voice, in your mind that sways
If you listen, close within
You can enjoy life with a grin.

I am the air, that blows you free
I am the water, smooth to agree
I am the earth, for all to be
I am the fire, don't mess with me.

I am a traveler, on this earth
God gave me life; He called it birth
He who keeps my sails free
In His Universe, just for thee.

When I follow His desires
No one will ever put out my fire
I listen intently, the inner voice speaks
He gave it to me to climb life's peaks!

ACKNOWLEDGMENTS

I feel abundantly blessed to share my story with you. Life has given me the ability to do so, and I am beyond thankful and grateful, in this life path, and purpose. Without my belief and trust in my faith, myself, and my Creator, I would not be here today. I thank you Lord.

I am also positively blessed with a supporting and loving husband. He has always had faith in me, and has awakened in truths with me. Thank you Al! I love you.

ABOUT THE AUTHOR

Lisa Leikam is like most people. She lives life taking it as it comes, in happiness and sadness, and in sickness and health. Believing it is the only choice we have. Up until a few years ago, that is.

Lisa's career started in 1978 as a chairside dental assistant, later transgressing into oral surgery, a profession she loved for 20 years. She became a licensed insurance agent in the state of Kansas thereafter, serving in this position for three years, before becoming a legal assistant.

Today Lisa is semi-retired, working part-time on a food truck. A fun job without the stress. She loves to travel, enjoys music and concerts, and spending time with her family. She is strong in faith, which brought her to this moment.

She is passionate about her spiritual journey, her new wellness and faith, and has a genuine desire to motivate and educate others. If you are interested in reaching out you can find Lisa at lisaleikam@yahoo.com.

You may follow her at:
Facebook at https://www.facebook.com/lisaleikamauthor
Twitter at https://www.twitter.com/magicladi
Instagram https://www.instagram.comawaken_capturedbytheholyspirit

References:

Page 9 Philippians 4:6   https://www.bible.com/bible/111/PHP.4.6NIV

Page 12 Peter 5:6-7 https://www.bible.com/bible/111/1PE.5.7NIV

Page 18 ACTS 18:9 https://www.bible.com/111/ACT.18.9NIV

Page 23 Dr. Beitman, Dr Beitman, founder of coincidence studies.

Page 31 Matthew 18:21-22 https://bible.com/111/MAT.18.21NIV

Page 35 Harvard Music https://www.health.harvard.edu/mind-and-mood/how-music-can-help-you-heal

Page 44 Jeremiah 33:3 https://www.bible.com/bible/111/JER.33.3NIV

Page 56 Psalm 91:11.1 https://bible.com/111/PSA.91.11.NIV

Page 71 Chakra https://www.merriam-webster.com/dictionary/chakra

Page 69 Transformation https://www.dictionary.com/browse/transformation?s=t

Page 82 Cherokee Proverb https://www.nanticokeindians.org/page/tale-of-two-wolves

Page 83 Fight to Flight https://www.merriam-webster.com/dictionary/fight-or-flight

Page 94 Consciousness https://waveofconsciousnessblog.com/

Page 84 Luke 12:22-26 https://www.bible.com/111/LUK.12.22.NIV

                     https://www.bible.com/111/LUK.12.23.NIV

                     https://www.bible.com/111/LUK.12.24.NIV

                     https://www.bible.com/111/LUK.12.25.NIV

                     https://www.bible.com/111/LUK.12.26.NIV

Page 93 The Serpent https://en.wikipedia.org/wiki/Serpent_%28Bible%29

Page 93 Fontana della Pigna https://www.ancient-symbols.com/pinecone

Page 94 Matthew 6:22   https://www.bible.com/111/MAT.6.22.NIV

Page 95 Laws of the Universe https://www.lawofuniverse.world/the-12-spiritiual-laws-of-universe/

Page 96 Nikola Tesla https://en.wikipedia.org/wiki/Nikola_Tesla

Page 96 Albert Einstein https://www.linkedin.com/pulse/everything-life-vibration-albert-einstein-rae-indigo

Page 99 Manifest https://www.dictionary.com/browse/manifest?s=t

Page 99 Mark 4:22 https://www.bible.com/bible/111/MRK.4.22.NIV

Page 99 John 21:14 https://bible.com/bible/111/JHN.21.14.NIV

Page 99 1COR 12:7 https://www.biblica.com/bible/niv/1-corinthians/12/

Page 99 Mark 11:24 https://www.bible.com/111/MRK.11.24.NIV

Page 99 Manifestation https://www.vocabulary.com/dictionary/manifestation

Page 100 The Word of Knowledge https://www.bible.com/111/1CO.12.8.NIV

Page 107 The Book of Genesis
http://www.vatican.va/archive/bible/genesis/documents/bible_genesis_en.html

Page 110 ACE; Adverse Childhood Experiences
https://www.cdc.gov/violenceprevention/acestudy/index.html

Page 112 Shakespeare https://literarydevices.net/to-thine-own-self-be-true/

Page 112 Magic - https://www.dictionary.com/browse/magic?s=t